Pleasant memories of the
Pastors' Institute, Springdale, Ark,
March 8-11, 1954.
The author
John Thomason

DEATH LOSES THE GAME

DEATH LOSES THE GAME

By

John D. Freeman

Author of

BURIED-LIVING

MORE THAN MONEY

TIME'S CHARACTER GAUGE

WHEN THE WEST WAS YOUNG, ETC.

MOODY PRESS

CHICAGO

To

My daughters, Georgia May Fielden and
Lucy Katherine White, whose questions and
unexpected comments as little tots set me to
thinking along lines which have found expression in these pages.

Foreword

As far back as I can remember I have been seeing pictures of Father Time in which he is usually represented as a tall, stately, bearded old man who has near at hand an hourglass and perhaps a set of balances. In such a role he has always seemed to be a twin brother of Death, who is pictured as a skeleton ogre with a sickle in his hand.

My conception of a proper personification of Time has changed with the passing years. Now I think of him as an indispensable director of life's intricate and complicated program. Instead of seeing Time as a grim old man, I think of it as an ageless sage, an umpire over the vast arena of life, punishing every violation with inexorable certainty and impartial justice, however inconsequential the breach may seem to man.

At the same time, I see him as a kind and considerate coach, who is always ready to give minute and accurate instructions to every player. Age after age he has preserved in the nature of all living forms basic characteristics and bents (instincts) upon which their perpetuity and welfare depend. And he has been even more considerate of man, for he has seen to it that representative incidents of human history should be preserved so that as a self-directing creature man would not need to go blindly on as generation succeeds generation upon the fields of action. Foolish, willful man suffers continuing hardships such as sickness, financial reverses, poverty, and strife, not because Time fails to provide instruction, but because of man's refusal to profit by what is revealed through the records left by his forebears.

Seeing the passing years impersonated as such a great-hearted, although stern and inexorable referee, I long since ceased to fear him. Instead of resenting his oversight and rebelling against his authority, I try to profit from his decisions. That this attitude toward the passing years brings much pleasure and great good, I trust may be seen in the autobiographical notes given in this book and the lessons deduced from them.

Time moves with steady, invariable tread. One who listens to an old-fashioned clock can imagine that he hears not the tick-tock of nursery rhymes, but the clomp! clomp! of a quiet giant as he moves about, keeping a never-shut eye upon everything and an unshakable hand in control of it. It should be encouraging to imagine also that this watchman is ever ready to impart information and advice to any rational being who will heed his message.

Time is the referee in the game between Life and Death. From him I have learned through a storm on Lookout Mountain to appreciate the peace and security which come to all who will know the Star of Hope toward whom all human records point. Tides and astral bodies Time has used to bolster my faith and to warn me against some subtle human weaknesses. A baby's questions and a lad's grim fears have been used to impart lessons of eternal significance. Fishing and sailing have furnished other valuable lessons. Such trivial things as a child's eating dirt and his curiosity about a silken cocoon in a fence corner have uncovered secrets about great spiritual verities. The old sage has used towering Pike's Peak for a pulpit, and the restless waters of a noted California resort to reveal significant and convincing testimony to the truth of our Lord and Master when He pointed out to a Hebrew scholar the one indispensable requirement for escape from sin's stronghold. The visions of the dying have made reasonable the instinct which points man to an endless existence in the spirit. They have removed all doubts regarding the fact of immortality.

8

Death has, because of Time's revelations, ceased to be a terrible specter from whom one should recoil in panic. No longer is he a bony ogre, wielding a terrible scythe. He is, rather, a worthy antagonist who plays according to the rules and, through his own opposition, brings added strength and increased years to every rational being who is willing to do what Father Time reveals as definite aids to victory. And all along Death knows that in the end, even though he shall have overcome the flesh, he will have lost the game, for the dying of the human body is merely the opening of the door through which a released spirit escapes temporal bondage.

It is good, therefore, for one to learn how to meet the attacks which Death is sure to make. If he does this, he may prepare for a triumphant end to the struggle by knowing how to be in "the way" and how to rely upon "the truth, and the life" (John 14:6), even upon Him who has "the keys of hell and death" (Rev. 1:18; 3:7), and whose final act while on earth was to conquer man's "last enemy," even death itself (I Cor. 15:25, 26).

J. D. F.

Nashville, Tenn., June, 1952.

Table of Contents

Illustrations

৩৩

POEMS

A Silent, Deadly Pack

CHAPTER ONE

Bogeys in the Dark

A Lad's Grim Fear

MOTHER, I want a drink of water."

A lad of nine years made the statement when it was time for him to retire for the night.

"Well, you know where the water is," replied his mother; "just run out and get a drink."

"I'm afraid," came the immediate reply, and it was made with deep earnestness.

"Afraid of what?" asked his mother.

"Afraid of the dark," was the answer, and it held a whole world of meaning for the lad.

The mother was a pioneer, accustomed to serious living and inured to danger. She did not, therefore, appreciate the child's fear of the darkness. Furthermore, parents in surroundings like theirs had the idea that children should be taught immediately the lessons they would need to know; hence, they seldom took time to explain in detail, or to lead slowly while the little one was learning. So, instead of taking the lad to her side and explaining what darkness is and going part of the way to the back porch where the water was, she simply made light of his fear and said, "If you want water, you must go and get it like a man."

The lad was not a man and at that time had no desire ever to be a man, if being such meant that he would have to go alone into dark places. He was, however, exceedingly thirsty, so made another appeal for the water, whereupon his father bade him go and get it.

There was no back talk in that home. When the parent gave a direct command, it had to be obeyed. So the lad went from the room with great fear in his heart. It was not so bad going to the well at the end of the long back porch, but his heart was thumping by the time he reached the shelf whereon the cedar water bucket sat. He quickly secured the dipper, gulped down several swallows of the refreshing draught, and then turned to go back to the living room.

It was then that the horrors of night became most real. It seemed that right behind him was a silent, deadly pack of creatures which he could not describe, but which he felt were sure at any moment to sink their claws or fangs into his back and legs. He sought to restrain his feet, but knowing that the porch and the open hallway were unobstructed, he suddenly made a mad dash for the door that led into the living room, skidded to a stop as he caught its outer knob, jerked it open, and entered, breathless.

"Now, you see, there was nothing out there to harm you," his mother said gently, but he lacked several years of being where he could see any such fact.

Growing older, the lad continued to be the victim of the phobia about darkness. He came to know there was no basis for his fear of it, but that gave him little relief. Even after reaching early manhood the annoying, often terrifying, sensation of being under the baleful eyes of some invisible ogre every time he was alone in a dark place persisted. It was not until he had spent weeks out-of-doors, sleeping on a cot under the stars, making

16

long hikes through the night, and spending long hours sitting in dark places that the fear was completely overcome.

What Makes Darkness Bad?

Behind one's fear of darkness is usually the impact of early training. The childhood of this lad was spent in a remote rural home. There he heard the usual pioneer stories about the wild animals and their attacks upon helpless human victims, especially upon little folk who dared go far from home. From a Negro neighbor, who cared for him and others of his family, during many days, he heard tales of ghosts, goblins, headless riders of the night, and other such ghouls. He lived in a community where parents and others made use of fright as a means of restraining children. To him the "Boogerman," "Old Raw-Bones and Bloody-Eyes," and other such creatures were as real as life itself; and they loved the darkness!

It was no pleasant thing to be in the open after dark and hear the voices of the night, which, where he lived, included those of the fierce and blood-thirsty as well as of the harmless. Most of the dangerous carnivore had been exterminated by the time he was old enough to be about the farm, but occasionally a panther made its way from the bottoms, a bear came near enough to raid the herds of wild hogs in the nearby forest, or a small pack of wolves came in from the Indian Territory. A few times he heard the fierce scream of a panther that was stalking prey in the forest or calling its mate. The howling of wolves was also heard. Such sounds made more real imaginary creatures which peopled the darkness.

Then, too, there were the obstacles against which one bumped or over which one stumbled and fell in the darkness, and they usually caused one to suffer. Even without the stories about wild creatures and bogeys, a child naturally comes to fear the dark, for it hides so many things from his eyes, holds so many causes of physical harm, thereby creating so much from which imagination may produce creatures that rob mind and heart of peace.

17

After I had passed the thirty-year mark in life, I was doing some work in Smith's Grove, Kentucky. One day a band of young people invited me to go with them to visit a nearby cave. Mammoth Cave is the best known cavern of the area, but there are many small ones well worth seeing. We went immediately after lunch, taking along a good supply of electric torches.

The entrance to the cave was roomy, and for some distance we walked upright under a high arched roof of solid rock. The floor was the bed of some ancient subterranean stream and was covered with a thick layer of fine sand. It was much fun following the course of the cave, exploring the nooks and crannies in its walls, and, of course, indulging in the usual bantering which is inseparable from buoyant youths. There were no dangerous side lanes or cross passages in which to become lost. At last, however, ceiling and floor came closer together. When it was no longer possible to walk erect, some of the party stopped. Others pressed on, stooping lower and lower until at last we reached a place where the ceiling was so low one had to crawl. At that point we stopped; most of the party were ready to turn back; but one hardy boy was not so inclined and challenged others of us to go on with him.

"There may be an opening up ahead into another cavern," he urged; "let's go on and see if we can find one. We would be the first explorers to do so; and, who knows? maybe the new cave would be named for us!"

No one else accepted his challenge, so, not wishing to disappoint the young fellow, I agreed to join him, and we started forward. The tunnel veered to the left, and before long we were out of sight of the lights behind us. The ceiling gradually lowered until even crawling became difficult. After we had gone several hundred feet and the space between ceiling and floor was less than two feet, the lad lost heart and decided he had

18

gone far enough. After finding out that I was not yet ready to stop, he left me and returned to the party.

I had had an idea which I wished to test out, hence desired to be alone. I wanted to see what it would be like in "outer [utter] darkness" (Matt. 8:12; 22:13). Slowly I wormed my way along, turning my head now and then and watching until the lad's torch had rounded the curve behind me and its flickering rays had disappeared. By that time I was almost wedged between ceiling and sand. I played my light ahead of me for a moment and found that further progress was impossible. I turned back and shouted, but my voice seemed to be caught in angry hands and thrown back at me before it could travel more than a few feet. Being persuaded at last that I was out of reach of every human ear and eye but my own, I snapped off my light and lay for several minutes in that impenetrable, indescribable darkness.

How much time I spent thus I did not check to learn. I wanted to retain the memory of the sensation of endlessness and infinity which came as I tried to examine that utter, absolute, soundless dark. It did not take a long time, however, to bring complete satisfaction. Soon bogeys which had tormented me as a child were being reanimated by my mind, and the creepy, crawling sense of enemy fingers reaching out after me returned. The man in me was rapidly reverting to the boy of old when I flashed on my light and started out, crawling from the restrictions which were beginning to make me once more the victim of a "nameless dread."

I was in no hurry to rejoin the party, so took plenty of time. Memories of childhood experiences came trooping out of their long seclusion. They called anew for consideration. They persisted in returning that evening after I was in bed. They started a chain of thoughts about the dark and man's fear of it. Why are we afraid of darkness? What is this strange phobia, and why does it come to harass our hearts? What good purpose does

19

fear of the darkness serve? These and other questions arose and demanded serious and continued study. Father Time has through the intervening years helped me find some answers.

The Cause of Fear

"It is quite natural," Father Time, the old sage says, "that one who has not been trained aright should be afraid of the darkness. In it he is, even when in a familiar environment, left much to his imagination, since he cannot discern with his natural senses what is about him. If he has been led to think of darkness as the abode of evil spirits, it is difficult for him to keep from imagining that such creatures are at hand. If experiences in the darkness have caused him pain or panic, he finds it difficult to keep from imagining that similar experiences are awaiting him every time he enters darkness alone. If, as should be the case, he has been shown the truth about darkness, he comes to appreciate its approach and senses in it another evidence of providential care.

"Nature's safety device which generates fear may be allowed to become a grim master holding a cruel rein upon the heart and will of everyone whom it can control. He who is afraid of the unknown will not venture upon untried paths, whether in research, explorations, or development. He who fears the unknown too much will never go as did Abraham in response to the call of God, or as did Moses when he returned to Egypt from his self-imposed exile. The instinct of fear is an instrument provided by the Creator to help preserve living creatures. It creates responses which make for security, and therefore insures perpetuity. But it can be allowed to dominate until it becomes a grim master of one's soul.

"However much one may be afraid of the things which he knows, fear of the unknown causes rational beings most pain and, unless overcome, proves to be one of their greatest handicaps. Things imagined are nearly always caricatures or distortions of the real with which we are familiar. The child who often hears stories about wild beasts and their night attacks upon helpless victims will people darkness with werewolves and creeping cougars. He who hears much about thieves, marauders and brigands will find darkness bringing about him such desperadoes. Whoever has lived such a sinful life that he often has been afraid of detection and punishment, inevitably struggles against grim fear that his Nemesis is just at hand. How much of mental anguish and sheer nighttime horror the current plague of comic magazines is causing America's children, psychologists are beginning to discover!

Dreading the End

"The masses have always been afraid of death, and the primary reason for this fear in man is uncertainty about what lies beyond the hour of dying. The darkness and dankness of the tomb create in any normal mind a subtle fear of what the silence of death brings; while death itself ushers man into a vast, unexplored realm of conscious existence wherein awaits us all that we most fear while in the flesh. Whoever, therefore, has not made sure that he will meet the Judge of darkness, with shriven soul, knows instinctively that he must face the tormentors and torments that await all the damned in Hades. Whatever one's ideas about immortality may be, he should be honest enough to examine the two principal things which inevitably bring grim fear to the heart of everyone who faces death:

"*1. Uncertainty about the Future State.* From more than one battlefield of every war have come reports of men, even the most skeptical and degenerate, who cried to God when the hounds of war were baying closely upon their heels, and the shrieks of wounded and dying comrades smote upon their ears. Modern warfare can cause thousands of fearful souls to crack up, many of them never again to become sane. 'There are no atheists in fox holes,' is more than an adage coined by a chaplain; it is a terse statement of a basic truth, for rational beings never face death, sudden or terrible, without becoming victims

21

of a fear which no human ideas and no amount of rationalizing can avert. If one is not absolutely sure that there are no terrors in the unknown realm beyond the grave, he can no more be without fear of death than the child of unwise parents can be unafraid in the dark.

"2. *Being Unprepared.* The greatest adventure upon which a rational being can ever set forth is dying. What does it mean? Why must it be? What happens to one's conscious self when death comes? What might one learn if death were to approach slowly and the brain remain entirely unharmed until the end? Why are people any more afraid of dying than they are of going to sleep? These and many other questions should be asked, for each deserves serious thought.

"When one makes a careful self-examination, seeking to find why he is afraid to meet death, he will, sooner or later, be found saying, 'I'm afraid of death simply because I've not made myself ready for the experiences which are an inseparable part of death. If I had taken time by the forelock and had done what every wise person should do, I would not only have arranged all my temporal affairs so that my going would cause my loved ones the least possible trouble, but I would have arranged my spiritual affairs so that there would be no question in my mind about the morrow.' Whoever is not wise enough to see that this reply is reasonable is not an honest student, but a prejudiced thinker who seeks not for truth but for an alibi behind which to hide when rational self clamors to be heard and obeyed.

When Darkness Vanishes

"It is a happy day in the life of any growing child when he can know that darkness of itself is not dangerous, and that tomorrow, although its content may be almost entirely unknown, is not to be awaited with fear and trepidation. Or, in other words, it is a big experience for a child to discover that there are playrooms and fairy lands in the dark, and that tomorrow but brings light with a new sun and a bit of added strength and wisdom with which to tackle what that tomorrow holds in store. Likewise, it is a happy day in the life of an adult when he can know that the unknown of itself is not dangerous, and that the future, even beyond the grave, holds adventures to challenge.

"Three things may be brought about which will banish fear of death and make a thrilling experience of the last earthly adventure which the spirit of man can know:

"*1. Turn fear into faith.* The instinct with which nonrational creatures are endowed must continue with them until the end, for without fear, the creatures would be destroyed, unless rational beings came to protect them. With man it is different. At first he fears to fall, but experience in averting falls leads to certainty of movements which in turn banishes fear. Fear of thunder and of the storm's crashing roar sends countless tiny tots trembling to the comfort of parental arms. But after awhile certainty that the storm is a beneficent agency drives fear away, and one leaves the open only to keep from being drenched with the downpour. Fear of one's fellow-being at first holds little folk at arms' length; but after a few moments together fear usually gives place to faith, and happy childish laughter tells the news. Likewise, fear of one's fellow-man holds adult men and women apart, leaving each a victim of imagined dangers as inherent in the other. It may create impassable barriers unless overcome. But once you refuse to be its slave, you begin to investigate, to experiment, to try; and before long distrust is gone, fear dies, and faith mounts to bring happy fellowship and fruitful relationships for life's big game.

"*2. Face the Unknown.* When one thinks of the shadows of death, he is at first repelled. The ignorance of what the shadows hold in store makes him see in them imaginary ills and ogres. He foolishly holds his inner self aloof from death and often vainly imagines it will help if he refuses to attend funerals or to look at the dead. He may continue this practice until his own end draws near, but he will by so doing make it more certain that he will go out into the dark terrified at what lies ahead. On

23

the other hand he will, if wise, become acquainted with death. He will never be foolish enough to try to run or hide from it. The powerful instinct to live will hold him in hand. He will not, however, shun death as if it were leprosy, but will seek knowledge of it.

"3. *Refuse to Be Enslaved.* He will refuse to remain a victim of the grim forebodings which the thought of death always brings to a wicked man. He will learn from the experiences of past ages that there need be no uncertainty about what lies beyond the valley of the shadow of death. He will not refuse to accept the testimony of the dying cynic of early Christian history, Julian the Apostate. Julian, having spent all his tremendous mental strength in trying to dethrone the Redeemer, cried in the hour of death, 'The Nazarene has conquered!' meaning thereby to acknowledge his own folly in refusing to accept Him as Messiah and Saviour. Again, he will not refuse the testimony of Stonewall Jackson, one of the world's greatest military strategists, whose last words were, 'Whether I live or die is all right; for whatever God does is right. . . . Let us cross over the river and rest in the shade of the trees.' Such a man will know no fear of the dark. Like the great philosopher and theologian, Paul, he will say, 'to die is gain' (Phil. 1:21). He will, long before death comes, have learned to dwell in the secret place of the Most High (Ps. 91:1) and will not fear darkness, whether it be physical or mental or spiritual."

Yes, Father Time has taught me to look at darkness that way. Whether darkness is produced by lack of physical light or by ignorance, it has the same evil effect unless one knows the truth. I am glad, indeed, that I did not ignore nature's warning when a lad, and that I have not failed to profit from my instinctive fear of the dark. I am much happier, however, because I set out diligently to find out and master the fear which darkness and uncertainty engendered. It was a great victory which took away forebodings and it saved me from continuing to be a slave of fear. God in His Word has taught me not to cower before the bogeys which frighten the natural man. Instead, I have learned to trust Him who is "the way, the truth," also the light, hence I have

NO FEAR OF NIGHT

Who is it fears the glum dark night
　　When death fore'er will close his eyes
And rob him of his mortal sight,
　　Of all that earth has made him prize?
'Tis he who's ignorant of the Way
　　To whom the shadows bring dismay.

Afraid of night? The tomb's bleak pall?
　　The dark that always lies ahead?
Ah, no! For long ago the inner call
　　For fellowship with God has led
My spirit out of Fear's grim sway
　　And made it free through Christ, the Way.

And now, instead of pain and dread
　　I look for joy and peace, for light!
No shadows blight the way ahead
　　For them who've learned to know that night
Is God's, as well as day—
　　For all who follow in the Way.

A Story, Daddy

CHAPTER TWO

Childish Prattle Points the Way

A Hungry Mind

"TELL ME A STOWY, Daddy," urged a tiny tot when, dressed for bed, she had climbed upon the father's knees and displaced the newspaper which he had been reading.

"All right," he replied, "what shall it be?"

"Anysing," came the immediate reply.

"What about Red Riding Hood?"

"No, not that. I'm 'fwaid of the bid, bad wolf. Tell me 'bout the white titty."

"Okay. Cuddle back, listen and watch.

> " 'Once there was a little kitty, white as the snow.
> In the barn she used to frolic, long time ago.' "*

The verses that have pleased little ones for three generations were recited all the way through to

> " 'When the teeth bit little mousie, Mousie cried out, "Oh!"
> But she slipped away from kitty, long time ago.' "

Eager ears took it in for the fiftieth time, and alert eyes fol-

* From "Long Time Ago" by Elizabeth Payson Prentiss, memorized from *McGuffey's Eclectic Reader*, Third Grade, more than half a century ago.

lowed the gestures made, then childish curiosity could no longer be restrained.

"What made the titty bite the mousie, Daddy?"

" 'Cause, little kitties like to eat mice. That's what they like to have for their dinner when they are hungry."

"What mates the titty hundry?"

"Well, let's see . . . how about another story? What shall it be?"

"Tell me 'bout the Ol' 'Oman," comes from excited lips.

> " 'There was an old Woman,
> Who lived in a shoe—' "

"No, not 'at ol' 'oman! The one w'at 'ad a doggie!"

> " 'Old Mother Hubbard
> Went to the cupboard
> To get her poor doggie a bone.' "

"What is a tubboard, Daddy?"

"That's the place where one puts the dishes and the food. Just like our kitchen cabinet."

"An' she didn't 'ave a bone for her doggie?"

"No, nary a bone, and the poor little doggie was hungry."

"Why didn't she go to the friderator?"

"She didn't have any refrigerator."

"Why didn't she git one?"

"Because she didn't have any money."

"I wish her doggie was here, 'count of I'd give it some of Bum's bones."

After a few moments of silence, a big yawn; then the sandman is at work, and a dimpled body is borne away to bed. Hanging to one corner of the crib is a toy monkey, a treasured possession only a few days old so still willing to run up its string when it is pulled. In another corner is a dilapidated teddy bear and near it a headless doll. Kneeling amid these treasures, she begins the evening prayer:

28

> " 'Now I lay me down to s'eep,
>   I p'ay Thee, Lord, my soul to teep . . .' "

"What's my soul, Daddy?" suddenly comes the question, and big brown eyes emphasize the seriousness of it.

"It's something inside you that makes you ask many questions."

"But *I'm* astin' kestions!" is the emphatic assertion.

"I know it. You are the same as your soul. You live in that body of yours and you use it to make yourself known. . . . But go on with your prayer, for it is past your bedtime."

"Where was I?"

" 'I pray Thee, Lord, my soul to keep,' " Daddy prompts.

> " 'If I should die afore I wake—' "*

Suddenly the prayer stops and up jumps the little tyke, electrified by a new idea. "Wait a minute; I want to show Dod what my montey tin do!" Forthwith, the monkey is forced to run up the string a couple of times, then she plumps down upon her knees, happy at the idea of having pleased God. The prayer ends, covers are tucked in, and a kiss silences the chatter. Daddy returns to his paper . . . but not to read! His thoughts turn from the affairs of his secular world to matters of eternal moment in the tremendous world of a newly arrived personality!

"*Who? What? Why?* Personality! Effect! Cause! There they stood before him, the three outstanding facts of rational existence. Already they had come before his little one and she had recognized them. Who did it? Instinctively she knew that there must be a creative person or agency behind every intelligible thing. The empty cupboard, the hungry dog—everything she met had its reason for being. No more could that developing brain of the little child believe that these things just happened

---

* The author has been in hundreds of homes, talked with parents of every kind, and he has never yet found one who claimed that anything but good ever grew out of teaching this simple prayer to a little one.

than she could believe that the toy monkey on her crib just came along.

One of the surest keys to knowledge about God and His ways was thrust before me; baby tongue had furnished the key. Eagerly I opened the door and stepped inside where I found Father Time standing amid endless shelves of musty books, and with the accumulated experiences of past ages at his disposal when he would reveal truths of everlasting significance. With ready will and hungry mind this musing parent heard the old sage talk about the instinctive or implanted knowledge which makes a little child so great a philosopher and theologian!

Immortality Assured

"Wordsworth was not indulging in idle fancies when he wrote the *Ode on Intimations of Immortality*," wise Father Time declared. "The poet-philosopher was expressing in a beautiful way a bit of profound truth which one cannot fail to see if he watches the unfolding personality of a baby. Its smiles must be accounted for. Who has not wondered at the radiant glow which often spreads over the face of a sleeping baby, even of one only a few days old? Surely the pleasure thus being evinced in dreamland must be connected with memories from another world, and must indicate quite clearly that the baby's spirit has come from God 'trailing clouds of glory' as the poet said.

"At the same time, how can one account for the baby's almost complete absence of familiarity with the body and the uses the body is intended to serve? Can the unusual mental and spiritual faculties on the one hand, and the gross ignorance on the other, be explained except by the fact that each human being enters the world at birth, as Wordsworth indicates, a dual creature, made up of a physical body and a rational spirit which is placed in that body, there to reside for a season, using it as a medium through which to find visible, tangible, and audible expression?

"One interesting thing about a developing baby is to watch it

30

as it discovers and learns to utilize various parts of the body. Oftentimes knowledge is gained at the cost of pain, as when hair is pulled out, or ear or nose is cut by untrimmed finger nails; what delight the little one sometimes manifests over a wiggling toe or finger!

"The parent is indeed foolish when he or she turns over too much of the care of the little one to nurse or maid or 'sitter.' The Creator provided certain instinctive responses from child to parent; these are never fully granted to others, especially during the months when imagination, the expression of the creative spirit within the child, is being turned from the glories just left to the physical realities at hand. To sit night after night and respond to requests and questions, repeated again and again, may be tiresome to a parent who knows nothing of the slow adaptation of the baby's personality to its new environment; but it should be considered as a priceless privilege, since it enables the parent to shape the course which the new spirit will take in life, to correct immediately errors in thought and judgment, and to help relate the child's soul to its body and environment in such a way as to preclude almost surely the dangers of having a 'problem child' at early adolescence, or a criminal at youth.

"If babies ever taught anything with definite and inescapable force, it is the fact that man's spirit is in his body but is neither of the body nor limited in action altogether by that body. 'Why?' any little one will ask ten thousand times, and always behind the question is implanted knowledge which leaves no doubt about origins. It seems to say emphatically and dogmatically, 'Somebody or something has to be hypothecated before a rational explanation for this or that phenomenon can be found.' There goes a mechanical genius, putting the last touches to a television set; there a chemical engineer at last finds the formula for sulfanilimide or penicillin; across the way an astronomer, aided by a physicist, finds how to analyze the soil of Mars and thereby to determine whether or not the planet can sustain vegetable life!

31

"We watch their work and we applaud them, usually thinking only of their physiques. Yet all the while—if only man would think—he would be seeing the bodies mainly as instruments through which immortal souls, created in the image of God, hence possessed of creative and directive genius, make known to others their thoughts and wills! Explain your baby's *who? what? why?* without knowing that the soul is an independent, rational entity which God made and placed in that dainty, dimpled body! It were far easier to explain the locomotive apart from Thomas Savery, Thomas Newcomen, James Watt, and modern engineers!"

God Revealed

So Father Time has brought a second lesson from the pleasant hours spent in happy abandon with the little ones while they were too unsophisticated to notice Daddy's foibles and faults, too innocent to bring the sharp sting of disappointment to a parent's heart, too naïve to cause heartache by willful disobedience. Again and again I seem to hear him saying:

"Man does not have to teach his children that God is; they know that by instinct. Just as the newly hatched alligator turns toward the nearest body of water, and the roots of a willow tree seek the surest source of moisture even when it is many feet away, so does the nature of every normal child, whether born in a Christian home or in a pagan hut, soon find itself searching for his Maker.

"Helen Keller tells of her reaction when, an avenue to her mind having been opened through her faithful and wonderful instructor, she first learned the name 'God' and what it means. 'I knew that all the time!' she exclaimed. How did she know? She had never heard one voice from without! 'Words' for her did not exist; yet she knew! She had discovered that inescapable fact exactly like other children do—because, having come from the creative hand of God, her spirit was intended for fellowship with God, hence led her to seek Him without whom her nature would forever be deprived of that for which it was especially endowed. Although housed in what had been a lightless, soundless prison, her spirit—the real Helen Keller—had held communion with God before she ever knew that He had a title and that others worshiped Him!

"The outreach of her mind and heart for God was purely instinctive, for she had no other source of information about Him except that which had come into the world with her. Many people who have had all their senses since birth, but were reared in homes where everything tended to prevent the so-called 'development of God-consciousness,' bear testimony to the fact of man's being made with as definite a bent in his nature for God as the swallow has for the air or the turtle for the water."

While working near Horatio, Arkansas, during the peach harvest of 1912, I spent much time with a youth of some eighteen years who had drifted into the camp and was pleased to find a friend. He came to trust me and finally unburdened a harassed soul. According to his story, some portions of which were subsequently verified, he had been deserted when two years old by a godless father who left him overnight in the care of a harlot in Fort Smith, Arkansas. His fallen mother had died, he later learned, and liquor had made a vagabond and criminal of his father.

Mother instinct in the proprietress of the disorderly house moved her to keep the dark-eyed, black-haired baby boy, and in her quarters he grew to be a sturdy lad. "You can imagine," he said in telling of the experiences which he could recall, "what I saw and heard around that house. There is only one thing in all the terrible picture that I would want to retain, and that is the memory of occasions when the woman I had been taught to call 'Mother' would come in the evenings into her private room where I lived, take me on her lap and rock me while humming some tune, often with tears running down her cheeks.

"If, during those years, I ever heard the names of Deity except in profane and irreverent uses, I have no memory of such an occasion. If, as occasionally happened, some girl started to sing what I later learned to be a gospel song, some other victim of lust would silence her with bitter invectives and profanity. I lived in that environment until I was past eight years of age, when I was taken in hand by a professional burglar who taught me to be his assistant. I recall my first time to enter a house from his shoulders and hand him things through the open window. And since that night until now, I've been like an alley rat, slinking, stealing, running—frightened all the time!

"But, Clerk, I also remember another side of myself which I have come to know again since being here with you. I do not remember when I didn't know God and talk with Him. Long before I had a chance to learn that profanity is wrong, or that there is a commandment against using the name of God in vain, I talked with Him after being tucked in bed by my foster mother, and left alone in the dark to listen to the roistering in nearby rooms. Somehow God seemed to fill an empty place in my room and to offer comfort and protection. I've never told this story to another, and I don't know why I'm telling it now, except that I trust you not to turn me in."

Other stories of the kind might be given, for there are many. One cannot account for faith in the existence of God merely by attributing it to the influence of environment upon a growing child. He has to go back of birth for an explanation, and when he does, he must admit one of two things: (1) the parents transmit to a developing fetus memories of their own thoughts and experiences, or (2) God gives the newborn a spirit which, as Wordsworth said, comes into the world "trailing clouds of glory from God who is our home." If one claims that the smile on a wee babe's face and the outreach of a little child's mind for God are due to memories inherited from the parents, he is confronted by the poser, "But how explain a case like that of the harlot-born, or harlot-reared youth?"

34

"One other lesson needs to be driven home to all Christians," Father Time said, when I later was pondering the matter of my baby's instinct for God, "and it should be dinned into the ears of the unsaved everywhere. That lesson is: There is no experience open to the human spirit so wholesome, so thrilling, so satisfying as intimate, heart-to-heart talks with God," and I know he was telling me another profound truth.

Far back, it now seems, I knew God in so close and intimate a way that I went to Him with as much assurance of His presence and His attentive ear as I ever went to my mother. On occasions when I wished to spend a night with some schoolmate, I would pray, "Dear Lord, make Papa and Mama let me go home with Will, or Ed and Sam, tomorrow night." If I needed something to wear or wished some other boon, it never occurred to me that God was not ready to listen to me. I talked with Him about my personal problems. One night, when I had been punished for misconduct and my brothers had taunted me about it, I went off alone and poured out my grievances to God, along with a torrent of sobs and tears. One evening when a pet lamb was dying of convulsions brought on by eating a poisonous weed, I watched it and dared tell God that He was not good to let the poor thing suffer so. But that was before I was eight years old!

This sin-calloused race needs sorely to be taught what it means for one to "turn and become as a little child." Science, so-called, has developed a chasm between man's soul and his Creator. Culture—often a misnomer for materialism—has brought man to feel self-sufficient, hence, to ridicule any idea that he needs God or should accept what his benighted spirit calls "the superstitions of religion, the panacea for the frustrated souls of the poor and incompetent." Yet, all the while there is an *emptiness* in every life that knows not God, and moments when the heart knows a longing which God alone can satisfy.

35

So Father Time has spoken much about the nature of man and his desperate need for fellowship with God by leading me to analyze some of the experiences which the babies brought me. Jesus, I now more fully know, did not mean when He said of little children, "Of such is the kingdom of heaven," that only tiny tots would be in Heaven. He meant that he who expects to inherit that kingdom must thrust aside all doubts about the reality of it and its triune God, must accept His instructions by simple faith and enter into its fullness and glory as a wee child who cuddles up in strong parental arms accepts his parent's assurances because of faith.

Somehow, the inescapable certainty of God, the tenderness and compassion of His great heart are thus more clearly revealed. It becomes more and more certain that man, although born of woman with a few troublous years before him, is nonetheless too important in the plan of the ages for death to annihilate. So, as the days pass, I find I'm growing more and more grateful in spirit and serious in heart. Some lines, written years ago in a school notebook, have come to have a new meaning for me.

MY PRAYER

Oh, lead me upward, Lord, to heights
From which I may behold
The matchless beauty of Thy face,
The boundless blessings of Thy grace!

And give me courage, Lord, to climb
Those steep and rugged heights
Which lead to Thee and life's great store
Of joy and peace forevermore!

Oh, show men fully, Lord, that they,
By climbing up the long, hard road,
Will gain at last a worthy prize,
Reward for every sacrifice!

CHAPTER THREE

When the Stars Go Out

Lost at Night

IT WAS A COOL, frosty night in early autumn. A new moon was
shining through a few filmy clouds which hung near the western horizon. Elsewhere, the skies were clear, and stars were
already bringing out their lights for the evening. An occasional
breath of air stirred the sear leaves among the branches of the
big oak trees near our house, strung along one side of the Rich-
mond-Cerro Gorda Road. Two of my brothers, Jesse and Henry,
and I decided that it was a good night for a hunt. Christmas
would soon be coming along and one source of our meager
Christmas "spendin' money" was the sale of furs which we took
after frost had come.

We asked Dad to go with us, but he was unusually tired from
a heavy day's work and, much as he enjoyed hunting, refused.
Against the protest of Mother, he suggested that we go alone,
since we had invited two neighbor boys to meet us for the hunt.
He went with us to prepare the firepan, gave the usual admonitions about care in felling trees, in avoiding starting a forest fire,
and about staying out too late. He then bade us, "Be sure to bring
home a big one," and watched us walk away into the night.

We Knew We Were Lost

We left the house with high hopes and unbounded enthusiasm. Drum and Sport, our "coon" dogs, were eager to go and rushed madly down the road ahead of us and off into the woods at the lane's end. We were not to begin hunting, however, until we had joined the neighbor boys at the Freeman School House a half mile away, so did not encourage the dogs in their first rush in search of a trail. We were at the school site in a few minutes, but waited in vain, for our neighbors did not come. After a half-hour or so, during which time our whooping and the tooting of the cow-horn bugle failed to bring any response from the direction of their home, we went back to the first farm, skirted its west fence and entered a vast woodland known as The Flats. Then we found some fat pine knots and replenished the flame in our firepan—a basket woven of steel strips and carried by a long wooden slat upon the hunter's shoulder. The great tract of timber contained sixty-odd thousand acres. It stretched westward from our community into Indian Territory (now Oklahoma). In it at that time was abundant game.

We had not gone far before the dogs struck a trail, and we eagerly followed them, thrilled by their vociferous baying. They soon treed, and we hurried to them. We found them baying up a small tree which we soon felled with an axe taken for the purpose. But when the tree-top crashed, the dogs found no quarry and, after scenting around for a few minutes, struck trail and bounded away with their vigorous yelping letting us know the trail was fresh.

Had our father been with us, he would soon have known what the dogs were chasing. But we were tyros then, and the bobcat —a species of wildcat—fooled us. A second time the dogs thought they had treed, a second time we chopped down the tree; a second time a brief search led the dogs off on another trail. The cat merely ran up the trunk several feet, jumped far from it, and made off, thereby causing inexperienced dogs to think he was up among the branches.

The hunt went on for about three hours, during which time

we went four miles or so into The Flats. We were so intent upon our quest for game that we paid no attention to direction and also failed to notice that the clouds were gathering thick. After felling a third tree, only to have the dogs pick up another trail and rush away, we knew they were not after a raccoon or an opossum, so decided to give up the hunt. The moon had long since gone down. The Seven Stars—compass of Heaven—had been hidden from us; but we never imagined we could not make our way without that pointer, so started in the direction we thought would take us home.

For about an hour we trudged through the woods, stopping only to find an occasional light'ood knot with which to replenish the light in the firepan. Then, suddenly, we came across the stump of a newly felled tree! "Isn't this the tree we cut down a while ago?" Jesse asked, and we found that it really was the same. However, it took a careful survey of the surroundings to convince us. Once again we set forth, determined not to go wrong a second time, but within less than an hour we were back at that tree! Each time we had gone in a circle which ended not ten yards from where it began! And each time we were amazed when we discovered what we had done!

The second time, however, made me know that we were lost. As the oldest, I had learned at school that when lost a person always moves in a circle. I tried to be very nonchalant when I told the other boys what had happened, but could not keep a note of alarm out of my voice. To be lost in that forest, wherein were some wolves and an occasional panther, was no small thing for lads as young as we were. In spite of my effort to be assuring, Jesse began to cry. Henry was seeking to quiet his fears, when suddenly from the branches of a giant white oak under which we had inadvertently stopped, there rang out a piercing, blood-curdling scream!

"A panther!" we cried in unison, and the hair on our heads started up. Tears again began to flow. We moved from under the tree. I recall quite vividly how I took a firmer hold of the axe handle, stepped back a few paces and bade Jesse stir up our fire. While he was doing this and I was standing guard, the cry came again, clear, penetrating, terrifying! We had heard stories of the call of a hunting panther, which is not unlike the scream of a desperately frightened woman. In the humid, still air of the forest it was natural to imagine we were immediately under a dreaded "panter cat" which was ready to drop upon us. But the second scream was followed by a weird, demoniacal laugh. Our hearts jumped with relief and joy! It was a horned owl and not a panther!

Our fright did not entirely subside, however, for we knew we were lost in a forest in which lived wild creatures and we had only a small chopping axe for defense. The remaining bits of our fat pine soon blazed up and we hastily gathered twigs and limbs and made a bonfire. We knew that the light of a fire would protect us even from the most feral beasts. Drum and Sport lay down nearby, their noses pointing away from the fire, each in a different direction—guardians they! When the blaze was going in a great, crackling way, we sat down close together. Our youthful minds began to tackle an age-old problem of the human family.

Why did we not pay attention to where we were going? Why did we get lost? When we were lost, how did it happen that we always came back to the identical spot from which we started in our effort to go somewhere? Why didn't something inside tell us which way to go, as it always told the cat or the horse? Of course, we could not answer these questions, but they persisted in returning. Father Time has brought me, during the intervening years, some valuable lessons.

Pleasure and Her Dupes

We young hunters were typical human beings, forgetting everything else in our eagerness to catch a "coon." Whither we were going, by what devious route we were getting there, how we were to find our way back—we had no time for such matters;

41

it was enough for us that our dogs were on a hot trail, that they were telling us the game had been treed, and that they were expecting us to come and get it! The excitement of the chase—an experience which any number of men, and many women, have known—pushed aside all thought of the hours ahead and what they might hold in store for us and our loved ones.

"So is it with foolish people in quest for fame and fortune," Father Time declares, "and for ease and pleasure. The quest is exciting; the lure of the coveted thing is strong; the anticipation of what success will bring is dominating; so poor, earthbound folk forget to watch where they are going. Soon they are lured into places where sin holds sway, there to be lost. They never consider how twisted and crooked oftentimes is the way they travel in seeking satisfaction for human ambition and carnal desires; so, before long, they are lost amid the things which appeal solely to the carnal nature.

"The 'certainty' that one more bit of speculation will bring a fortune leads some to send themselves to prison as embezzlers or bandits. The 'assurance' that one more step in sin will matter little leads many a youth to destroy chastity and thus to go through life, either blinded to the sacredness of purity, or else carrying a bit of inescapable remorse which memory will never let die.

"The rich farmer, about whom Jesus told (Luke 12:20) was a typical example of the millions of every age who think themselves wise and blessed if they provide stores of things which are to be used purely for temporal, personal pleasures. Jesus asked a significant question when He demanded of His followers, 'What is a man profited if he shall gain the whole world and lose his own soul?' (Matt. 16:26)."

Intellect a Poor Guide

Never was there a more complete and satisfying sense of right than that which was ours when we were circling through the woods on that memorable night. All the arguments in the world

could not have convinced us that we were not moving in a somewhat direct course toward home. If a compass had been handed
us, I think we would have doubted its accuracy. One may be
lost and not know it until it is too late; one may be lost and not
believe it, even after he has been furnished ample proof.

"There are countless lost souls in this world who are depending upon their intellects for guidance," Father Time asserts. "Little do they realize that the brain of one who is lost
is a poor guide out of the endless circle of sin. Such people
scoff at the idea of spiritual discernment. They ridicule the
teachings of God's ministers. They sneer when one warns them
of the end of sin's way. They insist that they are safe, that they
know where they are going; and many of them will never believe even their best friends who try to convince them that they
are undone.

"Let it be repeated with increasing emphasis," Father Time
seems to shout. "Conscience was never put in a rational being
to tell him *what* is right, or what is best for him; it can only tell
him *when* he is right. It is the navigator who will safely direct
the pilot, provided he has at hand sufficient knowledge of the
principles and regulations of spiritual flying. For one to believe
himself safe in the moral realm when he is ignorant of the Word
of God is as foolish as to consider himself safe at the controls of
a giant bomber when he has never attended a school for aviators
or studied a book on aeronautics. When Saul of Tarsus was on
the way to Damascus to destroy the Christians, his conscience
was altogether behind the move and assured him that he was
doing the will of God. But before he reached that city he learned
what a mistake it is to obey an uninformed conscience! (Acts
9:1–22; 23:1; 26:1–18).

"Likewise, when any person goes on in sinful disregard of the
fundamental precepts governing spiritual beings, precepts set
forth for man in the Bible, the revealed Word of God, conscience
has no means of warning him of his folly, no ability to make him
know of his perilous condition. 'I had not known sin but by the

43

law' (Rom. 3:20; 7:7) was Paul's way of setting forth this great truth. When one knows the law of God, conscience then has a basis from which to operate in bringing to him definite conviction regarding his conduct. Once let a person learn what The Book says about life and its needs, about conduct and its nature, about acts and their consequences, about guilt and its punishment, then conscience can speak with authority regarding his deeds. Until the truth is known, one need not expect to be made free from the errors which lead into continuing rebellion against God and right, hence, end in eternal night."

Lost Must Be Rescued

Nature reveals God to mankind, as Paul has declared (Rom. 1:18–26), so we can learn from natural agencies great spiritual lessons. We boys tried with all earnestness and persistence to get ourselves out of the woods in which we were lost. But at last we realized that our own efforts were futile; we must await either the rising sun or help from our father. Along about three o'clock in the morning the dogs suddenly pricked up their ears, one of them gave an excited yelp, and when we listened attentively we heard the faint tones of the hunting horn, coming from the direction just opposite to that which we thought would lead home. We sprang to our feet, rekindled a light in the fire-pan and set out, stopping now and then to get our bearings from the notes of the horn which a wise father continued to sound at frequent intervals.

Throughout the long, weary centuries men have been trying to devise ways and means whereby they may save themselves from the consequences of their sins. Great systems of idolatry have been devised, and the form of worship set up in them has been enlarged until numbers of parasitical priests and priestesses prey upon the ignorant, superstitious souls whose consciences are directed by the system of taboos developed for their control. Multitudinous gods have been carved from wood and stone and set up for the purpose of satisfying the inner demands

44

of rational beings for an object of worship. Various systems of ethics, philosophy, and theology have been born of man's desire for spiritual direction.

But through the ages and in spite of the many isms, there has remained in all who study with open minds a consciousness of something lacking; scholars of all ranks have recognized man's innate inability to get out of "the woods" and establish a right relationship with God. The lack is offset when men sit down midst their searchings and listen for the voice of the Redeemer saying, "I am the way, the truth and the life; no man cometh unto the Father but by me" (John 14:6). Heeding that voice, the anxious soul turns to the Bible and from that inspired record receives instructions which direct him to the eternal sacrifice for sin (Isa. 53:7; John 1:29; Heb. 10:10, 18, 26).

Joy in Being Delivered

Nothing short of the notes of Gabriel's trumpet to the ears of waiting saints will ever sound so musical as did the voice of the hunting horn that brought three boys to their feet that autumn morning. When we had gone far enough for father's voice to reach us, we discovered in it a richness and melody such as we had never before known. Peace like a mantle fell upon our troubled hearts when we at last had crossed the field and found rest and security in our comfortable beds.

Thousands of the redeemed of God testify to a wonderful joy in being "discovered of the Lord." Whenever one has discarded doubts, fears, conflicting emotions and wavering desires, has seen the hopelessness of one's efforts to redeem himself, and with penitent soul turns to the Lamb of God for spiritual direction, a new day dawns. Confusion gives place to order; doubt gives place to certainty; fright and suspicion are superseded by calm trust; the pessimism which creates all sorts of imaginary dangers is conquered by Christian faith; Christ is installed as Pilot; the will, mightiest factor in human development, is surrendered to the safest hands, and the happy believer can go about the business of living, finding increasing pleasure, until he reaches the port where fears, trials, confusion, temptations and all will be thrown aside as he enters into the rest of the soul.

"Yea, lost souls of men," Father Time pleads, "when you cease trying to rescue yourselves and are willing to listen for the voice of the Spirit of the living God, it will not be long until He will lead you to know the truth. Sensuous, carnal amusements and fleeting worldly gain will always keep you bound in a narrow circuit whose only exit is death. Slowly but surely, and as inevitably as the passing of time, you will wear away your body by pleasures which are found in gratifying the lusts of the flesh. Eventually your physical reserves will have been wasted, your body will be worn, its natural powers expended; then you will find that in ignoring the plea of the ancient preacher (Eccles. 12:1) you have squandered that which alone can add zest to living and have, thereby, closed the doors of hope in your own face.

"Why not be warned by Nature's witness to the inescapable fact that sin and selfishness never go in the right direction? Why not stop before you find yourself alone in the vast maze of a commercialized, mechanized world, not knowing what to do or where to turn? Why not accept the truth and enable conscience to issue true warnings? Why not obey common sense and, instead of beating further into the bush, stop where you are and listen to the call from God? As surely as it sounded in the days long ago, it sounds today. Repeatedly it rings across the ages and has lost none of its sweetness, none of its appeal. Hear it!

" 'Incline thine ear and come unto me; hear and your soul shall live' (Isa. 55:3); 'And ye will not come unto me that ye may have life' (John 5:40); 'Whosoever believeth shall not perish but have everlasting life' (John 3:16). Almost the last words in the inspired Book contain the call of the Almighty to all who are wandering in the paths of sin, blinded by the carnal nature, hoodwinked by Satan, going onward to a terrible, eternal doom. Listen to that call! 'The Spirit and the bride say, Come; and let him that heareth say, Come; and let him that is athirst come; and whosoever will, let him take the water of life freely' (Rev. 22:17)."

The old sage seemed to pause. I had time to think a bit for myself. From him I had received counsel for which I was grateful. I could trust his advice for he knows my nature, having seen millions of my kind. He knows my weaknesses for he has stood beside uncounted hosts who had like passions; he knows my needs for he has heard others who have cried out for help; he knows all men and would have them accept in simple, childlike faith the great truth embodied in these lines:

GOD'S WAY

The course of life seems good and plain
To him who's held in sin's strong sway;
Who, pleasure bent, will not refrain
From trav'ling his own sinful way.

The path is pleasant, free from care,
That leads one farther off from God.
Few souls thereon will e'er beware
The end where waits His chast'ning rod.

The trail which lures the carnal man
Looks good; but steadily it draws
Tow'rd endless night where nothing can
Console him who has spurned God's laws.

The carnal man goes blindly on,
Considers not where he may be,
Until at last, when hopes are gone,
He knows he's lost eternally.

The wise men wait and watch and pray;
The still small voice they gladly heed;
And, turning from their sinful way,
Find life and joy—reward indeed!

"The soul that enters the world with man is indeed his life's star," Father Time concludes, "and points him definitely toward God. But that star becomes weak with the passing years and fades out unless each one is warned by the Word of Truth and seeks the Lord while He may be found (Isa. 55:6). If this is not done, carnal desires, business cares, selfishness and its covetousness, worldly pleasures and lust will accumulate before his spiritual eyes, turning eventually into clouds of skepticism or agnosticism which inevitably rise to shut out the light that comes to the soul from God. When one is blinded completely by sin, nothing but a startling realization of being completely and hopelessly lost will jar a bit of sense into his head and turn his heart in anxious inquiry for help in getting out of the darkness on to the way that leads to Heaven and Home.

"You know what it means to be lost in the physical sense. You know how helpless one is when once the sense of direction is gone. The Creator put in animals an instinctive reach for home, hence without reason they move in a direct way toward home. But man is not a robot as are all lower animals; he is a rational being, and as such is capable of reading the stars; of studying moss growths, and of doing other things to discover ways of escape when once the sense of direction has been lost. Likewise he is capable of discovering the way out of the endless maze into which his carnal nature leads him. A father's call led the way out of the forest that memorable night. Even so will the call from God the Father lead anyone out of spiritual night and guide him safely into the security and blessedness of the heavenly Father's abode."

CHAPTER FOUR

Dirt Eaters

A Gruesome Sight

Mother, tommy's out by the chimney, eating dirt!"

This news was conveyed one summer afternoon in a loud whisper by five-year-old Henry, who was greatly agitated at having caught the little son of a visiting neighbor in the act of cramming a handful of moist dirt into his mouth. To him it was a startling discovery, and he could hardly repress a desire to shout aloud the announcement.

Tommy's mother caught enough of the whispered conversation to know what it was about. She was greatly embarrassed and said, "I don't know what to do with the child. He's simply crazy about eating dirt, and punishment doesn't do any good toward stopping him. When I first saw him doing it, I could hardly believe my eyes, for he has plenty to eat. Do you know what I can do about it?"

Did your mother ever make you take castor oil right off the spoon? Before pharmacists learned how to camouflage it, and when it was the cold-blooded autocrat of its particular field, people of all ages, especially children, came to detest the very name, and a threat to give a dose of castor oil was more effective in re-

TOMMY'S EATING DIRT

straining juvenile delinquency than was the prospect of being switched or spanked.

Yet there are people who thoroughly enjoy castor oil. One neighbor of ours had a daughter from whom the oil bottle had to be hidden. A Negro, who often worked on our farm, took delight in telling children that when he could get it, he ate castor oil on his bread instead of syrup. His pantomime, when he described pouring the oil into a saucer and sopping it with a hot, buttered biscuit, is a very vivid part of memory's store. He, like the girl, had overcome the initial revulsion to the oil and eventually there had come in its place a craving for it.

During two summers of my college days, I taught the Flat Creek School between Allene and Foreman, Arkansas, living in the home of Richard Wright, an uncle of my mother, a veteran of the Civil War, and a successful farmer. Of all the many incidents of the days spent in his home, one picture was indelibly fixed in my memory. Each morning during the first summer, when we were seated at the breakfast table, Uncle Dick picked up a large bottle of quinine, which was always at his place, poured a small mound of the fluffy white powder upon the palm of his left hand, and then licked it with his tongue, and swallowed it without aid of liquid. I watched him go through this ritual for several mornings and finally asked, "Uncle Dick, why don't you put that quinine into capsules, or at least wash it down with some black coffee?"

I can see him as he sat there, tall, thin, wiry, and strong in spite of his years and of a crippled lower limb, the result of being hit by a Yankee minnie ball. His eyes twinkled and a smile spread over his face. "Oh, if I did either, I'd lose the flavor of the quinine," he finally said.

"You don't mean you like to taste that stuff?" I said, greatly surprised.

"Why not?" he replied. "I've taken it so long without any 'doctoring' that I have come to like its flavor. My breakfast wouldn't taste just right without it. You see, one can bring him-

51

self to where he will enjoy almost anything, if only he keeps on trying."

In these days when it seems that the whole race is bent on becoming victims of things against which Nature has sought to safeguard us, it is time we were paying some attention to her laws and to the penalties she exacts of all who violate them. Often during recent years I have been made to wonder at the terrible way people have allowed their appetites to become lust, and the sorry extremes to which so many go in gratifying this debased instinct. God gave hunger as a necessary safeguard; but in civilized lands, it is rapidly being converted into lust which money-mad owners of commercial agencies and institutions are using to fatten their purses while leading an increasing number of foolish people either to kill themselves or to handicap themselves for life by weakening vital physical organs.

What real difference is there between the dirt-eating lad of my boyhood days and the youths of today who use tobacco? What is there that leads one to revolt at taking castor oil, yet makes him think it "smart" to boast about drinking or of getting away with a number of cocktails? Why should one who smacks his lips over a quid of tobacco think himself qualified to call another person a heathen because the other human being eats raw snails or live grasshoppers?

Civilized people should be aroused to the dangers inherent in prostituted natural desires. Nature has her very definite methods of protecting her creatures. She has put within them instinctive reactions against that which is harmful. Man alone is able to overcome these. He alone willfully thrusts aside the safeguards in his desire for temporal pleasure. Only man eats curative herbs when his body is not ill; he alone diverts from their God-intended mission such things as caffeine, nicotine, alcohol, and opiates, and allows them to make a slave of his body, thereby robbing his soul of the only instrument it has through which to make effective its creative powers.

Through a good many years of observation, out of numerous

personal experiences, and by means of many hours of study, Father Time has made very plain some important truths upon which Tommy, Uncle Dick and others set me to thinking.

Nature Yields Ground

"A thing quite clearly seen by one who is observant is the certainty with which Nature yields before the insistent will of man," I hear him saying. "Whether the tiny tot overcoming a natural revulsion against dirt or the mature adult breaking restraining bands against alcohol or nicotine, one takes the same steps. Her safeguards are slowly worn down, and at last they seem to have disappeared altogether. In most instances man, having broken that which was intended to restrain, finds in its place an unnatural desire or lust which completely enslaves both body and will."

While a college student, I once lived in a home where dwelt a young woman who was as delicate as a hothouse flower. Her skin seemed almost transparent; her body, although perfectly formed, was thin and extremely frail. Upon meeting her I was struck, as other students were, by her fine spirit and pleasant mien, but was distressed because she was so delicate. The reason for her physical weakness was soon evident, for not only did she use too much condiments with her meals but usually topped off her very meager food with a teaspoon of salt, black pepper, and vinegar, which she swallowed with evident relish, often taking a second dose during the evening meal. Being a country boy, hence unshackled by authorities on etiquette, I took advantage of the first time we were left alone at the table to ask her about this strange habit.

"Did a doctor tell you to take that mixture?" I asked.

"Why, no," she replied with very evident surprise. "What makes you ask that?"

"Well, I can't figure why anybody would take a dose like that without being compelled to do so," I answered.

"But I really enjoy it," she said and smiled.

53

"Don't you know that eating that stuff instead of wholesome food will kill you?" I asked with rural bluntness. "How long have you been doing this?"

"I don't know that it's any of your business," she replied, nettled at my presumption. But she added, "I don't know how long I've been doing it. I guess I learned by degrees to crave it."

"Well, it's about time you were quitting it," I said frankly. "Anyone with the talent you possess should treasure her body too much to feed it vinegar instead of milk. Please don't be offended at my frankness, but I must say you are very foolish not to put an end to a habit like that, when it is so evidently making an invalid out of you."

Fortunately, she saw the folly of her course and quit the harmful habit in time for the necessary restoration of her body. Today, she is a useful, charming matron who draws dividends from her victory.

One may run roughshod over any barriers placed about him for his protection. Beside many a highway extends a sturdy fence or wall designed to keep motorists from running off a bluff, but one occasionally sees where some driver has crashed through the safeguard. Few people ever like the first taste of alcoholic beverages. Most people react violently to the stronger alcoholic content of distilled liquors, unless they are diluted and dressed up by skilled hands. The first tobacco produces nausea or extreme dizziness, or both. But once obsessed by the idea that one must smoke and drink in order to be up-to-date, it will not be long before the barriers set by Nature will be breached and the things intended for one's welfare will have become slave bonds, hard to break.

"The unfortunate thing about it," cries Father Time, "is that victims of alcohol or nicotine, more than any others, are so completely captivated by the physical pleasure derived from use of it that they not only are unaware of the organic changes which are taking place within their bodies, but resent any suggestion from a friend, even from a physician, that trouble is developing. Furthermore, these victims are prone to build up a 'defense mechanism' that leads them to resent any criticism."

God Repeals No Law

Another vital lesson which Father Time presents to all who will hear is the certainty that Nature never repeals one of her laws. The fact that the foolish person is unaware of the incapacity creeping upon him through gratifying an abnormal appetite in no wise removes the danger. Usually, the victim not only ignores the source of danger, but resents the effort of a friend to warn him against it. The violent opposition of a drunkard to every attempt to take his bottle from him is an illustration, showing the terrible hold which alcohol eventually takes upon one's body and mind. The extremes to which a cigarette user will go in order to secure another "fag" can be learned from any honest habitual smoker, especially from veterans of recent wars, who had to spend long periods where cigarettes could not be easily obtained. Thousands of heavy smokers can tell of the mad craving for a smoke which tempts one to pick up a cigarette butt from the street for one "drag" on it.

Surely Father Time has made it very certain that one who "enjoys" the relaxation of a series of smokes, or revels in "the freedom from restraint" which alcoholic beverages may give is also suffering certain inescapable organic adjustments in his body, each of which is produced by Nature's effort to rid his body of poison, or else to fortify the flesh against it. The victim of any habit, whether eating dirt, indulging in excess condiments, or being a slave to poisons such as alcohol, nicotine, and opiates, denies that he is being injured by it; but that does not change facts or postpone the inevitable day of judgment which is approaching. Eventually nerves become so sensitive that the smoke no longer brings relaxation. One cigarette, failing to satisfy, is crushed out; before its remnant is cool, another has taken its place between the smoker's lips. One drink, whether beer, wine, or distilled spirits, failing to produce the desired reaction, is followed by another and another. Even carbonated drinks may be used until an abnormal desire for them has been created and one has become a "coke" slave.

And all the while reserves of the body are being sapped. The heart works a bit faster because of caffeine, alcohol, or opiate. It finally begins to complain, revealing its rebellion either by periodic bursts of speed or by skipping its regular beat. Eventually the reflex nerve centers, which control the action of the heart, become weary, their reins are slackened, and the poison-maddened pump either quits outright or becomes so enlarged (angina pectoris) by excess work that it causes its owner violent pain and makes him incapable of normal living. The lungs, their delicate tissues having been hardened by the continuous effort to help rid the blood stream of its poisonous content, find work more and more ineffective, hence slowly fail in their function, and lung cancer increases at an alarming rate!

Occasionally, one sees an exceptionally strong man—rarely ever a woman—whose physique withstands the ravages of sin. Victims of the harmful habits are foolish enough to think such a person offers proof that indulgence in narcotics and stimulants does not hasten death. Thus a noted inveterate pipe smoker, who from the time of his service during the Civil War had never seen "a day pass without taking one or more toddies," is still mentioned in an Arkansas community because he lived to be ninety-three years old. But no one refers to the scores of men who died between thirty and fifty because of heart failure! No one refers to the number of alcohol-nicotine victims who pass out suddenly while yet young because of pneumonia or tuberculosis. Sinful man wants an alibi for his sinful indulgence, hence, ignores all facts which reveal to him his folly. Father Time seeks diligently to make him know that there is no way to escape the application of an eternal, universal law, namely, "He that soweth to his flesh shall of the flesh reap corruption" (Gal. 6:8).

"Fritz, why don't you quit all this nonsense and give God a chance?"

A godly deacon at Allene, Arkansas, asked the question one day long ago. Methodists were conducting a revival meeting, with an unusually able minister doing the preaching. Interest was running high, and many Christians were working. The man to whom the deacon addressed his question was a big, florid fellow of thirty-five years—a happy, jolly man, but extremely profane, a cigarette slave, a tippler, and a gambler.

"Oh," he replied with a sneer, "don't worry about me. When you are as strong as I am, then preach to me about my way of living. I get too much pleasure out of my fags and drinks to turn them loose just because you church people are against them."

He persisted in his opposition to the church. No amount of persuasion moved him. A few months later he was caught in a rainstorm; his body was thoroughly drenched and chilled; pneumonia developed; within forty-eight hours he was dead! "Nicotine and alcohol sapped his heart, and it would not stand the strain of the disease," was the physician's verdict. In any cemetery one will find many a grave whose marker would read, if the epitaph told the truth: "Here lies one who thought he could fool Nature by turning alcohol [caffeine, nicotine or an opiate] from its God-ordained mission to gratify his carnal lusts." Or: "She thought she was having fun when indulging her appetite. What she was really doing was digging herself a premature grave."

What a terrible price anyone pays for the temporal pleasure self-indulgence brings! Tommy enjoyed his dirt, but it was killing his body! Uncle Dick came to where he enjoyed quinine, but if he had allowed himself to use it as many people use nicotine or opiates, it would have killed him within a few months. He used it, as Nature intended he should, only as an antidote for malaria and according to directions from a capable physician.

"One may sneer at a child that has formed the habit of eating dirt, and classify him as a moron," Father Time declares. "He may speak of the folly of becoming a drunkard, a cigarette slave, or a dope addict, and try to account for such stupidity by asserting that the individual thus afflicted 'lacked stamina of will.' He may accept the modern liquor maker's false theory which states that it is as well to be an alcoholic, since so to be prevents one from turning to some other form of self-indulgence. He may accept the propaganda of those who reap enormous profits from the manufacture and sale of numerous harmful products—drinks as well as so-called foods—and become an enemy of every organized effort in society for the suppression of businesses which depend upon the debauchery of mankind for profits. He may do all in his power to make others believe that there is no harm in a 'friendly, social drink'; nothing about a cigarette to cause one to worry; nothing to fear from overindulgence of any kind except 'excess flesh which proper diet and exercise will reduce.'

"But no arguments can disprove facts; no ignorance can change Nature's course or bring from her any leniency when she applies the penalties for violation of her laws. 'I have set everything in its place,' she is forever saying. 'Use it as I intended and it will prove a blessing to you. Prostitute its use for the sake of any temporal pleasure it may bring, and I shall exact full pay from you—long days with quivering, pain-wracked flesh for every year of foolish, sensuous delight.' "

Freedom Assured

One other lesson should be kept in mind. Father Time has written it all over the world. The scar on the bark of a growing tree; the twisted skin tissues on the body of a victim of burning or scalding; a sixth sense or increased powers of the sensory nerves of a blind person; the cartilaginous sac formed about a needle which remained for months in a child's body; the ready adjustment of the left hand to tasks imposed when a right hand has been lost—these and numerous other things bear witness to the willingness and readiness of Nature to restore any damage done to the human body, or to provide some substitute for what is damaged beyond repair. Even so is God ready to heal the diseased spirit of man and restore the will to its rightful throne.

He was at death's door. Delirium tremens had come for the third time, and it had converted him into a madman. His wife had escaped in time to save the life of their baby son against whom alcohol had turned the father with a maniac's hatred. I had been called by a neighbor of the man and shortly after dark had reached his home on West Kentucky Avenue. What a scene for a young pastor to face! What an experience through which to pass! Let psychologists explain the case without acknowledging divine intervention, if they can!

I remained during much of the night. I talked when I felt that conversation would be profitable. I spared him not, but described his sorry condition as graphically as I could. With the authority of the physician behind me, I told him emphatically that he was bound for Hell and would be there in a few minutes if he ever suffered another attack of delirium tremens. I pictured his lovely young wife, running down the street in utter terror, holding their baby frantically to her breast, seeking shelter from a husband-father who was fool enough to let a saloonkeeper sell him stuff that made a maniac out of him. I told him in plain, blunt words what would have happened to him if he had killed his baby.

And he heard! At times he cried out from genuine anguish of spirit. The verbal castigation hastened the return of sanity. He was led from seeing devils without to contemplate the demon within that had made him so vile.

The rest of the story is one of a heroic fight for freedom. The man turned from his former work in a distillery and from his

59

former companions. For weeks he walked several blocks out of his way to avoid passing a liquor store. Within six weeks his wife and baby were at home with him. He soon professed faith in the Great Physician and became a member of a church.

The lust for alcohol was finally conquered! One of the most thrilling of all my pastoral experiences came when, about a year after his "last spree," as he referred to the near fatal spell, he came to me one Sunday morning before service and said, "Preacher, I'm all right now! Yesterday, I went into a saloon at Twenty-eighth and Broadway and made Charlie go home before spending his week's wages for liquor; and I took him by a grocery store to see that he spent it for food!" "I came; I saw; I conquered" never meant more to Caesar than this report of triumph meant to that lowly laborer!

I know a man who smoked for forty years until his heart began to go bad and his eyes were greatly weakened. With God's help he quit the habit when he was nearly sixty years of age. At seventy the "ticker" was beating with regularity and precision, and his eyes were growing stronger. Thousands of former alcoholics have come from their enslavement, and Nature has gone a long way toward restoring strength and health.

A childish hand wielding a toy axe some twenty years ago slashed the tender bark on the only yellow poplar tree in Ashdown, Arkansas. Ten years later one had to have a keen eye to detect the spot where the gash was made. An exuberant grandson of the late Chancellor Bruce Payne, of George Peabody College, Nashville, Tennessee, then a lad of six, was swinging an old, rusted, tin bucket when the pail broke loose and the sharp, rough brim of the pail cut an ugly gash in a little playmate's forehead. Five stitches closed the wound, and after five years had passed almost no scar marked the place. Time again holds forth words of vital importance to man!

"Just as Nature rebuilds the outer shell of trees or replaces the skin of man," Father Time says, "even so will she work to rebuild the broken, marred, weakened inner man, once the will

60

to forsake sinning has been formed, and fellowship with the Great Physician has been established by faith in and reliance upon the Word of Promise. Being an innocent victim of sin does not cause ruin; else Christ, who became sin on our behalf (Rom. 8:1–4), has forever been abased. The shame comes in being so enslaved by sin that no longer is there a desire for freedom! There is no dishonor in having been stricken by physical illness; the shame comes, first of all, in having ignored or willfully violated Nature's laws, or in the second place, in refusing the remedies which Nature has given to protect us from the effects of illness, once it has been incurred.

"The willingness of Nature to restore a broken body is God's testimony to His readiness to heal and restore that which is marred by sin. So the spiritual being who was intended for fellowship with the eternal God need not be a helpless prisoner of a body so degenerate that it enjoys eating dirt or indulging in unending use of alcohol, nicotine, opiates, or of less dangerous but naturally repulsive things!"

My mentor ceased and left me again to my musings, and I began to see that there is desperate need throughout the world for a crusade to emancipate the hordes of "dirt-eaters" who are a terribly expensive burden on society. From far beyond the Flood which once purged the earth, down across the passing centuries, one may discover from human records many warnings which Time is continuously issuing against the folly of intemperance, or more accurately, against the sinful lack of self-control.

One may also learn from these records how truly the Creator desires every rational being to keep unspotted from the world, to guard himself against the tendency of the flesh to accept and then demand that which, although created for beneficent ends, may become a destructive force, sapping both physical and spiritual energies, thereby marring the divine image and bringing impotency and failure to that which was created for eternal ends.

THE FOUNTAIN IS CLEAN
(Psalm 32)

Blest indeed is the man, whosoever he be,
When his sins are all freely forgiven;
When their blight and their stain are all taken away
By God's grace, through Christ's blood which aye cleanses.
He's released from hard bonds when his soul is set free
From iniquity's slav'ry and shame.

What renown is the man's, wheresoever he live,
Who no guile in his heart will let tarry;
And whose thoughts, guarded well, come with beauty and strength
That ne'er fail to arouse admiration.
They're not soiled with the lusts of the world and the flesh,
They're the product of sanctified brain.

He who bridleth his tongue must begin with the heart,
For from it are the issues of living.
Guard with care every door that to it opes the way
For the fast-flowing tides of man's thinking.
Let the words thus be born of a mind that is free
From the blight of profane, obscene thoughts.

Be ye glad and rejoice in Jehovah, your God,
You who trust and obey the Redeemer!
Loving-kindness shall compass your way, guide your steps,
While the wicked shall know many sorrows.
So with care, guard your life, keep your heart clean and free,
And be ready each hour for God's call.

CHAPTER FIVE

Thor Hurls His Hammer

A Storm on Lookout

DID YOU EVER SEE a storm gathering under you as you stood on a mountain, or rode in an airplane?

Everyone who has been fortunate enough to witness such a scene has had an experience which will stir any but a confirmed Stoic. It is one thing to watch a storm cloud approaching when you are below it; it is entirely different to be above it and watch it crawling along the earth, seeming to reach out mighty tentacles and embrace bit by bit the ground and all that it holds.

One evening during the late summer of 1932, I stood alone on the brow of Lookout Mountain, Chattanooga, Tennessee. Not far from me were the silent guns which once belched death and destruction into the ranks of the Federal army which was seeking to scale those rugged heights. The night was black as ink, save for the lights of the city far below me and the occasional bolt of livid fire which broke from an approaching storm cloud and thrust aside for a split second the impenetrable gloom which shrouded the crest of that mighty bluff.

It was as still about me as the inside of a tomb, save when the distant thunder rumbled across the valley and echoed from cliff

THOR HURLS HIS HAMMER

to cliff until Missionary Ridge, seven miles away, finally caught its waning strength and flung back the last echo. The flashes of lightning showed great boiling mountains of cloud approaching from across Moccasin Bend in the Tennessee River, and the brighter flashes illuminated the vast dismal scene, causing one's imagination to picture in the ensuing darkness massive piles of crumbling masonry, just ready to topple down upon Chattanooga which lay peacefully in the valley below, with its myriad street and window lights looking somewhat like giant glowworms, among which auto lights like fireflies flicked about.

Standing there that night on the great boulder from which many hundreds of thousands of tourists have looked with delight, I lived in a world altogether different from what the average person knows. For some time it seemed that the cloud would pass under me, but as it drew nearer to Lookout, the upward currents of air caught its belly, lifting it until it became quite evident that Lookout Point would feel the full fury of the storm's blast.

I waited, however, quite assured, because there remained almost directly above me a rift in the clouds through which one weak star shot its feeble rays, timidly anxious, I thought, for the creatures below. It was the one thing which seemed cheerful at that hour and offered assurance. As long as I could see it, I had time to get to shelter in a nearby shop before the rain would descend.

The eerie stillness which pressed closely upon the heels of every jolt from what my primitive ancestors thought to be Thor's hammer came to have a depressing effect upon my spirit. Some faint remnant of the long-lost instinct which had already sent the lower animals to cover made me uneasy in spite of my judgment. Reveries, however, soon captured my attention and I found myself trying to analyze the emotions which surged up within.

What is there about a storm to make one feel that he is in

the presence of a supernatural being? How does it come to pass that unhampered natural emotions arise in the presence of any mighty demonstration of Nature's power, bringing the certainty that there is a realm of the spirit no less real and tangible than the natural realm of which the human body is a part? Were our pagan ancestors and the rest of the heathen world wrong in believing that spirit powers created the storm, caused life to awake in the springtime, brought about changing seasons and other such recurring mysteries? Is man acting with sanity when he deliberately ignores the instinctive response of his soul to the voice of God, uttered through the manifestations of Nature?

"God would speak to rational beings everywhere through His other book," Father Time reminded me, "if only men were not too unwise to hear. Instead of accepting what the inner man asserts to be truth, vain man discounts the value of information which comes through intuition. He sees how unerringly this knowledge leads the lower creatures; but when it points him to a supernatural source of all that he sees and knows, then he grows rebellious and will have no such guidance.

"When one stands face to face with any unusual phenomenon on Nature's vast stage, there is, unless repeatedly inhibited by stubborn will, a spontaneous inner reaction which brings definite satisfaction to the inquisitive mind of him who watches. Why then are people foolish enough to discount such spiritual reactions by suppressing the instinctive desire to worship the Author of the wonders that thrill their souls?"

I had lost myself completely in my musings when there came an unusually brilliant flare of light followed almost instantly by a terrific crash of thunder. I turned my eyes upward to where I had last seen the star, and it was gone. At the same instant a bolt of white fire crashed through the air not far from where I stood and shot downward to strike a tree a thousand feet below. I could hear its sizzling passage as it sped athwart the mountain top, bent upon a point of contact with the earth below, from where its mystic counterpart drew with stupendous power.

It struck! A terrific piercing crash followed! The thunderous roar bounded from Lookout with a second boom little less pronounced than the first had been. The echo jumped back from the face of the cloud which had almost reached the mountain, then it leaped up from the ground far below, and finally came back from Missionary Ridge which was already being washed by a deluge of rain. Another flash of light, and another mighty detonation followed! The storm seemed to challenge the right of the mountain to continue standing as it had done for so many ages. I turned and fled along the trail, going as fast as I could with the aid of the recurrent lightning. I reached a curio shop just as the first great drops of water, among which large hailstones were intermingled, came rushing down.

What Price Paganism!

On Lookout that night the cloud was right about me. The air itself seemed to be dynamic with the energies which work together to form the raindrops. The massive piles of natural masonry which form the brow and bluff of a great mountain helped to make more effective the play of the storm sprites.

The swishing, rattling, hissing demons were soon lashing their wet mops against the windows of the curio shop. The rollicking wind steeds dashed around the building, throwing hailstones, like gravel from shod feet, upon the roof, and rushing past to be followed an instant later by another charging company. For several moments the lightning was so continuous that there seemed to be a gigantic floodlight fixed upon the top of Lookout. The thunder rolled and bellowed across the valley, echoing back and forth between the mountaintops, until one could imagine himself as a helpless spectator of a mighty artillery duel between invisible spirits of the powerful armies of the Blue and the Gray, competing once more for possession of Lookout Point.

Timid souls are terrified by such a scene! Those who love Nature when she is in a tantrum get a reaction seldom, if ever, found elsewhere. It startles! It intimidates! It awes! It makes one aware of his infinite littleness when set up alongside the mighty forces of Nature. Yet, withal, it sends shivers of exquisite pleasure through one's soul, and instinctively the Christian finds himself humming:

> God moves in a mysterious way,
> His wonders to perform.
> He plants His footsteps on the sea
> And rides upon the storm.

"When your primitive ancestors passed through such a storm as this," Father Time seemed to say, "they knew not God, hence had a different reaction to that which you now enjoy. Victims of the misinterpretation, placed by their priests upon the revelation which the Almighty has given man through Nature, the Angles and Saxons of the British Isles, the Normans and Teutons of western Europe, and the Norsemen from up the way, felt sure that the wild rampages of Nature were expressions of anger on the part of one or another of their gods. You should appreciate the sentiment which led the Teutons to account for the destructive lightning and the crashing thunder by creating a god named Thor whose mysterious hammer caused the recurrent noise and destruction. In the flashing of lightning and the crashing, rumbling thunder, the primitive man saw his imaginary theophany expressing the rage of his gods against the earth, and his spirit was awed and afraid.

"There are millions of people throughout the earth who are still so enslaved by ideas which have come down from pagan sources that they are unable to realize the difference between their fancies and the facts which I have long since established. One such person turns to fickle science to account for what he

68

sees and senses. Another turns to other human beings with a false assurance that they have the means of access to God, hence, can offer protection. He readily accepts as his spiritual intermediary some man or woman, follows in the train of such an imposter, or turns with the mind of a child to accept the ritual upon which some group relies for income, and through which poor, fallible man is held in mental slavery.

"When the trials of life beset such people, storms gather about their souls and troubles harass their spirits, they know not the soul-liberty which enables one to sing in the shadows and rejoice midst a storm. Not knowing the Ruler of nature, they miss the thrilling experience which comes to everyone who knows that the storm's wrath provides a bath for land and air, softens the face of the earth and makes way for a brighter and happier tomorrow. One pays a terrible price for being a pagan; one pays even a heavier one for being a victim of materialism or of ignorance and superstition while living among those who have discovered the full, rich, exalting revelation of the Almighty.

"You are but a few generations removed from a people who were held in the grip of a pagan religion," the old sage added. "How wonderfully blessed are the offspring of the Saxon, the Celt, the Norman, the Norseman! What a debt they owe to the daring missionaries of centuries long past for braving the natural rigors of the country to which they went with the Gospel! It was a big and lasting victory which some of these adventurous souls won one night when they challenged the superstitions of the Druid priests and slashed the tree which was the alleged abode of their chief pagan god!"

The Upward View

The storm brought anew to my attention how good, how very good it is to be able to look upward through the clouds which come along life's way, in the midst of the sorest trials, during the hours of greatest stress and strain, even when the foundations of one's hopes seem crumbling away like ant hills before the tread of a mastodon—how good it is then to be able to find a rift in any cloud and see shining through it the Star of Bethlehem who is forever saying to everyone who trusts Him, "God is faithful, who will not suffer you to be tempted above that which ye are able; but will with the temptation [testing, whatever its nature may be] also make a way to escape, that ye may be able to bear it" (I Cor. 10:13-b).

"As long as you are able by faith to see the friendly face of the Son of Man through the gloom," Father Time continued, "you can know that all is well with you. You can be assured as was the Psalmist, 'He that dwelleth in the secret place of the Most High shall abide under the shadow of the Almighty' (Ps. 91:1). The clouds may gather about your spirit. Troubles, distress, sorrows, heartaches, loneliness, even despair may pile up and thrust their daring, often blasphemous, queries through the gloom to harass a distressed soul; but to know that the Messiah is here, even when the cloud shuts out His face, will always bring an assurance which nothing else in the ken of man can provide. As long as you know that He is above the clouds, no fear can master your soul.

"You are now enjoying a thrilling experience which most people never know, for they either cannot or will not pay the price of visiting the wonder spots which Nature has placed over the earth. People live twenty, forty, even seventy years within a few miles of Mammoth Cave, yet never go inside that wonderland to see its vast, silent auditorium, its petrified pipe organ, the lightless river with sightless fish. You have done well to come here; you are fortunate indeed in having come tonight. 'Tis worth making a long journey to see such a spot; 'tis worth waiting long to be here during a storm!

"But how much more of the real meaning and purpose of life do they miss who never take advantage of the opportunity presented by the Creator to enable rational beings to know Himself and the power of His eternal Spirit! The nonbeliever sees only the outward, often the terrifying, aspects of a storm; for, like a primitive worshiper, he knows only the instinctive reactions to the spectacle. Having disregarded basic spiritual facts revealed by Nature and having refused to open his mind and heart to the simple, direct, convincing story of the Gospel, he knows little about the natural realm of which he is a part and less about the Friend and Brother of everyone who desires His fellowship; thus he goes on in utter disregard of the future, and when some storm breaks about his soul it finds him unprepared, unprotected, hopeless, despairing!"

Thus did Father Time speak. In recalling his message, I am reminded of a tragedy, with the aftermath of which I was connected. It happened one day in southern Arkansas. I was called upon to conduct the funeral service of a United States cavalryman who had committed suicide. The young man was an orphan, his mother and father both having died when he was yet a lad, leaving him and a sister to face life as it came. Because they were bereft of parents, they readily came to feel dependent each upon the other for some things which parents alone give in full measure. After becoming a man the brother enlisted in the army and was assigned to a cavalry unit with which he had spent several months. Then one day a letter came telling him that his sister had died a week before and had been buried beside the parents in a country graveyard.

In a moment the world went bad! Dark, cold gloom settled about his soul. Doubts filled his heart with startling and terrifying suddenness. The dread clamor of warring forces within disturbed his mind. Before him there was only night, a long, cold, friendless, loveless night which offered no single consolation to his troubled spirit. He went listlessly about his duties for the remainder of the day, and that afternoon, while returning from the parade grounds, he slipped a cartridge into his rifle, put its butt into the stirrup of his saddle, placed the muzzle against his ribs under the heart, and pressed the trigger with the toe of his boot! Because he had not found a haven for his storm-ridden soul, his day of despair ended in the eternal night of doom!

It is indeed a grievous error, a mistake of eternal moment, when one goes into life so bent on making money or on having fun, or so concerned about winning in some contest with his fellow-man, that he forgets the end of life and all that is involved in it. Ignoring spiritual things, he loses contact with the Invisible who helped us build air castles when we were young and who enabled us to plan for noble adventures. Just as I, that night on Lookout, became so interested in my musings that I forgot to keep an eye upon the star above me, even so do people become so engrossed with the cares and pleasures of life that they fail to set life's compass by the Star of Hope. Thus God who wooed them so readily and so strongly when they were children and youths finally departs from their way. When storms come, as they inevitably do, these people have no source of light to guide their steps.

"Everywhere, men need to be reminded again and again that the Almighty provided for each animal form a place of protection and an inner witness to the existence of such a place," Father Time assures me. "The lowly earthworm pushes deeper into its burrow when the soil about its home is disturbed. The little chick rushes to the protection of its mother's wing at the appearance of danger. The newly hatched alligator or turtle moves unerringly toward its home in the water. Creatures of the woods know where their havens are to be found. Thus the hare runs for the hollow in the tree, the squirrel climbs to the branches above, the bobwhite nestles amid the fallen leaves.

"God has not left man without security or without a natural desire to find it. It is not a matter of survival of the fittest; it is the persistence of them who most clearly discover the place assigned them in the Creator's plan and who most thoroughly learn to know and do His divine will. Man has always known fear of physical harm and how to find some degree of security when danger arises. He has always known fear of spiritual hurt; but all too often he has not used his common sense to the end that protection against the forces of degeneracy and evil

72

may be found. Instead of cultivating the desire for fellowship with the Creator, he lets the lusts of the flesh enslave his will and when, like the poor victim of delirium tremens, he most desperately needs God, he finds about him an array of foul spirits taunting his defenseless soul!"

The storm on Lookout, hurling its fury against the crest of the hoary mountain, aroused in me some of the native fear-complex, and with it came the commanding need to seek shelter. And study of the sensations experienced that night led me to know more surely the importance of one's seeking shelter for his spiritual nature, a secure covert for his soul when the inevitable storms of life strike about it. Just as I found physical security inside the stone house that night, even so did I long ago find complete freedom from spiritual fear by taking shelter in the Covenant of Grace. So the Psalmist's expression of faith, "I will lift up mine eyes unto the hills from whence cometh my help" (Ps. 121:1) has grown meaningful to me.

LOOKING TO THE HILLS

Through tall, rock-crested hills I hear
The Psalmist's voice ring, rich and clear,
"Lift up your eyes! Let heart draw near
That Rock who banishes all fear!"

The mountains grand—each rugged hill—
Reveal to man what God's good will
Doth offer all who trust Him, till
His holy purpose He fulfill.

Assurance comes from each bold peak
That God will shelter all the weak.
Encouragement the hills bespeak
For them who peace and comfort seek.

Then trust His pow'r! Whate'er He say
Believe! When He doth ope the way,
Securely led, our spirits may
Look calmly toward each dawning day.

73

Since 1770 astronomers have not seen Lexell's Comet. It was lost, they now claim; yet, according to calculations of the eighteenth century, it should have reappeared every thirteen years for world folk to see. What became of it? Did it burn itself out in stellar space? If so, what became of the matter into which its original form was converted, if matter is indestructible? Did it come too close to some mighty planet and have to yield to its attraction, thereby being drawn into its titanic embrace? Or did its "elements" melt with fervent heat, its atoms disintegrate, with the result that a spectacular explosion occurred somewhere in the universe? Who knows?

This strange interstellar vagabond, so brilliant and spectacular for a season, is a fitting type of each god whom men have worshiped during various periods of recorded time. Each idol came into view because of the limited mental vision of some pagan priest or scientist (medicine man). Each heathen god attracted local attention for a season. Now and then one such deity inspired high ideals and lofty thoughts which endured because some follower recorded basic moral truths which he attributed to the imaginary deity. But, as Lexell's Comet flashed and then disappeared, so does every man-made deity eventually disappear and his worshipers turn to some other person or object for satisfaction of the inherent religious impulses.

Baal and Molech blazed their names throughout the ancient civilized world. One or both were worshiped by the masses of the Near East, and their dread names inspired fear along the eastern borders of the Mediterranean Sea. But they are gone now! Woden and Thor were not creations merely of priests; they were the best efforts of Teutonic minds to express convictions forced upon them by implanted knowledge within and by Nature without.

Woden and Frey, Thor, Ceres, Astarte and others are symbols of man's search for Truth and of his insatiable hunger for God.

74

He has to worship; therefore, without the specially revealed truth, he gropes in the darkness of pagan night and finally sets up an image which, at least to some degree, satisfies his hungry spirit. That no such god and religion ever fully satisfies is attested to by the continuous struggle of non-Christians to attain a clearer vision of God than idols and ritual and priests can provide.

Once again I seemed to hear Father Time calling to me: "Hopeless indeed is the state of the millions of China, Japan, and India, and other countries of the Orient. They have been robbed of their pagan gods. No longer do their priests have an acceptable panacea to offer them when they are in trouble. No longer do the graves of their ancestors constitute a shrine before which they can find satisfaction for the religious instincts which God planted deep in the nature of all rational beings. Their temples are being torn down or turned into storehouses, or places of sordid amusements. Their spiritual stars have proved to be erratic comets and are being lost. Unless they are shown the Day Star from on high, the Bright and Morning Star, the darkness and distress of mind and heart which they have known for ages must increase.

"Who can hear the roll of the war drums, think of the flashing might of modern war machines, and contemplate the awesome, appalling might of harnessed atomic energy and not have his heart go out to the helpless, bewildered masses of the earth in such a way that he will not be able to resist the call to send them the Gospel that they may not be left utterly alone in the shadows and storms of the way? Who, with any sense of values, would remain aloof from the Christian missionary enterprise, when the distressed masses of the world are mutely evincing the utter hopelessness of unbelief, nonbelief, skepticism, agnosticism, and infidelity? The new day which radio, television, air transportation, and world integration are ushering in dooms all pagan gods to extinction. Who can estimate in any accurate manner what that means to the teeming masses of pagan lands, unless the Christ of Calvary is revealed to them so that the ever-lasting Father may supplant the fickle gods of the past?"

The Hope of the Ages

As I stood atop Lookout Point that summer evening and watched the clouds gathering, I felt the presence of the Almighty in a new and definite way. There I learned more thoroughly something that has meant much to my soul during the succeeding years which saw the passing of loved ones and the end of the generation that brought me into the world; years that brought a third upsurge of world-wide greed and cunning, political graft and crookedness, with international conniving and pillage on an unprecedented scale; a period that saw a third outburst of hate's terrible scourge, with mechanical monsters doing the bidding of shrewd and daring men, with the result that havoc, such as Tartars and Huns of medieval days could not even imagine, was turned loose upon the earth. Again Time spoke with commanding authority:

"Above all powers and principalities, above all stress and storms, high above the level of any human attainment, and supremely greater than any gods man has ever imagined, Jesus Christ reigns supreme in the Christian firmament! He is the Star that will never be moved! He will never change or grow dimmer. Passing years cannot affect Him or alter His beneficent ministry to men. Through Him mankind has had a true and complete and final revelation of the nature of the eternal I AM, the God whom all people know to exist and for knowledge of whom the best minds of every generation since Adam have struggled. He is the Star that guides innumerable mariners on life's voyages. He is the Pole Star that points the way for the traveler through the deepest woods, across the loneliest deserts, on the widest sea, out of the most dismal morasses and jungles! He is the Light that lighteth every man unto the way that leads to eventual spiritual triumph.

"No fickle comet He! No vagary of human superstitions He!

No figment of the imagination, no variable satellite of some greater deity! He is the Alpha and the Omega, the *Categorical Imperative,* the *Raison d'Etre* without whom all origins are veiled in eternal darkness. He is the *Alpha* of species, both natural and spiritual. If one seeks to go back to the beginning without the guiding ray of His eternal mind, he inevitably travels into a *cul de sac* beyond which lies only mental night. He is the *Alpha* without whom every human mind faces enervating, disturbing agnosticism, or hopeless skepticism, when he seeks for the ultimate cause of his own existence and his intelligent, creative spirit.

"He is the *Omega,* the end without which man's visions prove to be colossal hoaxes produced by mental indigestion, a tragic illness brought on by contemplation of mysteries which grow into incomprehensible miracles, unless man can by faith see the ultimate aim and end of rational existence. Jesus Christ is the Goal toward which every normal, natural, informed man is drawn whenever he allows his mind to contemplate the future for which he was made, and with an instinctive longing for which his spirit is endowed by creation. He is the end of sorrow and distress, of fear and anguish, of selfishness and greed, of hatred and cruelty, of sham and falsehood.

"He is the Prince of Peace, without whom the world of our day would be hounded by the increasing dread of what war and man's hate can produce in another quarter century. He is the end of life's faint dream and blurred vision. Man is always blessed when he turns from the foolish fantasies which carnal minds generate, listens seriously to the inner voice which from earliest memory has told him of God and made him realize his need for fellowship with Him.

"When a rational being holds fellowship with his Creator through study of the Word of Life, through contemplation of the mysteries of Nature and through intimate prayer, he will soon find that all clouds of doubt will melt away, and from the East to the West, from the North to the South—everywhere he may turn his mental eyes—there will be the clear and bright assurance that all is well. The storms of life never catch him unprepared whose actions are determined by the light which is given to the world by the Son of Man."

THE MORNING STAR

O Star of Hope! Thy gladsome ray
Doth scatter darkness, though the day
   Have died in hours of starkest gloom!
The light of life doth from Thee flow,
Though storm clouds black may hang below.

O Beacon Star! Thy radiant light
Doth offer guidance, though bleak night
   Have closed about my troubled head.
A beam of hope from Thee doth glow
E'en when naught else the way can show.

O Star of Life! Thou brilliant ray!
My stay in hours of stark dismay
   When Nature fails to comfort me!
I'll let my compass point to Thee
And fear not what the end may be.

CHAPTER SIX

Swelling Seas and Shining Stars

Tides at Long Beach

ALL OUT of the surf!"

The warning came from a lifeguard at Long Beach, California, one day during July, 1915. The weather was ideal, the surf unusually good; consequently, a large number of bathers were enjoying the long, lazy swells which had been coming in all afternoon.

Most of the bathers responded immediately to the call of the lifeguard, for they were residents of the area and were familiar with the whims of the great ocean. Some visitors, however, did not know and, not having had their fill of the sport, continued to ride the swells. A second warning brought all of these out except two venturesome youths. Ignorant of the danger that was creeping between them and the shore, they continued to enjoy riding the swells and running in on an occasional breaker. The guard left them alone and one of them, taking it easy upon his back, was caught in a strong undertow which had developed. Before he knew it, he was on his way out of the bay. His first intimation of what was taking place came when he noticed the pier approaching him quite rapidly, and knew that he was

Singing Through

Sometimes days seem long and dreary;
Other days are short and cheery.
Some days bring the heart real gladness,
Others fill it full of sadness.
  So, I'll ne'er feel glum or lonely
  Though paths be dark, or shaded only;
  For I'll lift my eyes and see
  Something good awaiting me.

Sometimes days are filled with sorrow,
But I'll know there'll be tomorrow
When the pain will turn to pleasure,
Joy be found that knows no measure.
  Every cloud has silver lining,
  So I will not sit a-pining;
  I will lift my voice in praise
  E'en through the darkest days.

While the stars above are singing,
Bird songs all around are ringing,
Why should mortals yield to sorrow?
Why be fearful what tomorrow
  May hold out for us to face?
  God is watching, and His grace
  Will not fail, though long the way,
  But can gladden every day.

Keep my soul, O God, from fear!
Let me cringe not when I hear
Things that tend to cause alarm,
Things which threaten me with harm.
  Every day I'll gladly face
  If by Thee I hold my place;
  Then I'll bravely go my way,
  Singing through the darkest day.

drifting. He was a fair swimmer and physically fit, so by dogged effort he won out against the undertow and finally reached the shore, but only after being thoroughly frightened by the drag of the current which has swept many surf bathers to death.

By sunset the tide had risen more than five feet and breakers from ten to fifteen feet high were rolling in. When each big one struck the sea wall, a deep, hollow "boom!" resulted, sounding like the firing of a ten-inch coast artillery piece during night target practice. And each boom was accompanied by a mass of water hurtling high into the air, scattering great showers of salt spray about it. The scene was awesome to the landlubber, who watched until night had drawn her curtain over it and his friends began preparing to go home.

"What makes the sea so rough?" I asked one of the friends.

"The moon and the wind," was the reply. "The tide is unusually high this week, due to the phase of the moon; the strong wind pushes in a lot of extra water."

I knew enough about the moon's attraction to understand the "Why?" of the tide; I did not know enough, however, to be prepared for what I was witnessing. A few days before in San Diego, I had seen demonstrated a device which its inventor claimed would harness the power of the waves and utilize it in pumping sea water into a great tank from which it would return to the sea through a turbine, thus turning an electric generator.

"What kind of pump could withstand the impact of these waves? What machine could harness that?" I mused while watching the seas crash against the sea wall. "And what kind of equipment would be required to anchor the pump where the greatest power could be secured in operating it?" Who indeed could estimate the unfelt power of the moon, silent, cold mistress of the night, forever pulling at our planet with her invisible fingers, exerting a force that would probably never have been known by man, had not the rising and ebbing of the seas along the coasts started inquisitive minds in search of truth?

Ten years later that youth, grown to be a mature man, was on a college campus with a professor of astronomy as his companion. It was almost midnight. The autumn day had been clear and crisp. A telescope had been set up and the professor was opening some fascinating mysteries. He focused the instrument on Saturn, and then turned it over to his guest who got a glimpse of the planet as it slipped out of focus.

"What happened?" I asked, wonderingly; "I saw something but it quickly moved away!"

The professor laughed and said, "Yes, it did move away. The telescope remains in focus only a brief while, for, you see, we are turning away from Saturn at a high rate of speed. You'll have to learn to use this gadget so as to follow a star with this magic eye."

He showed me how to operate the telescope, and I soon learned to hold its "eye" upon any heavenly body. Then far into stellar space I reached, pulling toward me things never before seen by my eyes. Saturn was enlarged to show very clearly her mighty halo, her far-flung rings of illumined gas—or is it atomic energy in process of becoming visible matter? Jupiter, titan of our Solar System, came close enough to introduce some of his train, seeming to take especial delight in his bewitching moons. Sturdy, rugged, cold, and heartless Mars stood forth showing his canals—or are they mighty ramparts built by warring Martians?—probably constructed by some superrace such as were the Anakim who once inhabited parts of our planet (Num. 13:22, 33).

What beauty one can find in the heavens! No wonder the ancient Egyptians studied them and built up their systems of astrology! No wonder the Psalmist was inspired by the heavens which reveal the glory of God! (Ps. 19). No wonder Clyde Tombaugh's soul was inspired by contemplation of the stars when he was a lad on a Midwestern tenant farm! What virile boy, possessed of a fertile imagination, could study the heavens through one of our mighty, modern telescopes and not begin to dream about making exploratory trips into interplanetary regions, using a rocket space ship to discover what goes on "yan side" our known spot in God's vast abiding place!

Once again curiosity—that wonderful hunger of the human spirit for knowledge—was aroused, and questions were thrown at the professor. "What are those glorious rings about Saturn? What produces them? Are they always in the same relative position to our planet, or do they sometimes stand on edge like a vast balloon tire with Saturn as the hub? How are they held in place? Can people on Mars—if indeed that planet is inhabited —see them? What sets Jupiter off to himself, alone in a vast area as he seems to be? Are his moons similar to our moon, only cold, bleak, dead planets forever encrusted in ice? And what about Mars? Does he really exert a baleful influence upon mankind, making him bellicose in spirit? If people live on Mars, what are they like? And the North Star! How explain it?" Later on there arose another interesting question about this "lone wolf" of interplanetary space: "Is it possible that it may be the center and control station of all interrelated universes, the 'proton' about which move vast magnetic 'neutrons,' each carrying in its embrace a planetary system?"

The chain of questions, started that night, when for the first time I saw the heavens greatly enlarged, is still stretching on. I could then have asked a thousand questions. To some of the first ones the professor made reply; to others I have found answers elsewhere. While we dismantled the telescope, put it away and went on to my room in a dormitory, the professor talked. How much of his speech memory reproduces and how much has been added from other sources I do not know, but standing out in my mind are these observations:

"We are learning a great deal more rapidly than was possible until man learned to harness the mysterious energy which we call magnetism. Father Time has not let us idle away all the precious days! Now, with our giant electric-controlled telescopes which move automatically with the split-second precision of the distant heavenly bodies; with the material and equipment which physicists and chemical engineers have developed; with stores of information secured by translators from the writings of ancient Egyptian and Babylonian astronomers and astrologers; and with hosts of things discovered during this century, man is able to reach far into the inexhaustible treasure chest of Nature and bring to light marvels which cause the greatest minds to jump with eager delight and to renew with increased vigor their search for truth.

"The greatest handicap the race has had to overcome in pressing this search has been the almost unbreakable hold which fixed ideas have upon man's mind. Once the scientist, whether he be an Aristotle, an Archimedes, an Einstein, or a savage medicine man, has succeeded in persuading men that his theory—hypothesis—about any evident great fact is true, it is a serious task to bring them to question the validity of the theory, and a more difficult one to lead them to be willing to discard it if it is shown to be false. If men of religion, whether high prelates of an established church or simple preachers of the backwoods, accept the theory as a fact and incorporate it in their theological system, the task of destroying faith in it becomes all the more difficult. Man has been misled by theories far more often than he has been guided aright, yet the theory must come in order that the fact may be established. Truth, especially about nature, springs full-blown only on rare occasions.

"When Columbus had disposed of the flat-world theory, and Pasteur had eliminated the last ground for the idea of spontaneous generation, the fallibility of scientists was exposed, and the vainglory of the 'scientific mind' was clearly revealed to all who would profit from the revelation. Today we find in some places scholars trying to cover the weaknesses of ancient science by putting upon the religious leaders of the past blame for the long ignorance about the shape of our planet and the persisting superstitions about the origin of life; yet those ancient men of religion—with the exception of the few scientists among them—merely accepted what they were taught, and then sought to defend it as truth! Today we see science turning sharply away from the Darwinian hypothesis of organic evolution, but in all too many cases we see the men of religion holding to the outmoded theory, ready with caustic tongue or pen to ridicule those who never accepted it in place of the Word of God!"

Sleep did not readily come that night and, with the morning, questions came again demanding further study. A text on astronomy was secured and the subject was reviewed. The matter of tides gained new meaning, and interest in the vast stellar empire grew. Now, after several years have passed, I venture to pull the whole "portfolio" out of memory's store. From the data may be drawn some conclusions which Father Time has forced upon me.

Pleasure's Lure

"The lifeguard on any public beach is a necessity," he declares. "Not only is he called upon by some who are seized with cramps, or who unexpectedly find their strength gone; he must also watch out for those who become so engrossed with their sport that they stray too far from the shore, or otherwise jeopardize their lives by forgetting that danger may creep upon them even in comparatively shallow water. Whoever expects to enjoy the surf in safety without having on hand a competent lifeguard doesn't know the sea.

"How like pleasure-seekers everywhere is the ordinary surf-bather! Foolish, rational beings become so enamored of a good time, so bewitched by a few moments of exciting pleasure, that they ignore what Wisdom has sought to give them and all that Experience would add from her store. The two of you who risked your lives at Long Beach for the sake of a few more moments of sport were in no sense different from countless others. Your recklessness merely emphasizes the folly which leads so many people, especially young folks, on in their search for sensuous pleasure. Many who live by the sea play on, ignoring the possibility of approaching danger until too late, and in like manner, hosts of pleasure-bent human beings go on ignoring the warnings which the Creator has set about them and, when too late to recover themselves, cry in vain for help.

"When a flood threatens to inundate their feeding grounds, wild deer, bear, and other beasts of the forest heed the warning which Nature gives them through the mysterious 'inner voice' called instinct. As soon as they are fully fledged, migratory fowl are drawn together by an invisible power and begin training for the long flights which save them from extermination. Fish sense in advance the approaching storm and leave the shallows where rough waters would endanger their lives. Even the lowly razorback hog responds to Nature's warning and builds, hours in advance of a coming blizzard, a snug bed of brush, leaves, and straw.

"But poor, self-willed man long ago refused to be guided by Nature, so most instinctive safeguards have been lost. Furthermore, the warning voices of specially chosen prophetic souls are ignored or openly derided by the pleasure-bent masses. Lifeguards along my shores of time, who know enough about God and His eternal program to be able to foresee impending calamities which the race sooner or later must meet, are too often swung away by Madame Pleasure, and so do not notice the approaching perils. They who cry out against the dangers inherent in the increase of drunkenness, adultery, profanity, Sunday desecration, gambling, divorce, human greed, and class strife, are ignored. They know from study of history and by the authority of God's Word that social revolution with great destruction of life and property will come in the wake of such degeneracy, as inevitably as a high tide and wild breakers follow a 'near' moon and strong wind.

"The vast array of heavenly bodies, moving in an endless parade of indescribable power and glory, tells mankind of the inescapable nature of the laws which the Creator had to establish before He could have an orderly universe, or order, harmony and continuity anywhere in it. The same Mind that set in motion the forces which brought Nature into being also set up forces which produced and maintain a spiritual realm. The physical is necessary to give expression to the spiritual, and at the same time it enables the Creator to convey to the spirits of men vital messages for their good. Since man has no instinct to warn him of impending spiritual troubles, he sorely needs to bring himself into intimate relations with God's eternal Spirit so as to have near at all times the Spirit of truth (John 16:13) who will never leave unwarned any soul who yields to His infallible direction. Many people are drowned each year on unguarded beaches. Millions of souls are doomed each year, some because there are no spiritual guards to warn them, others because they are too foolish to hear when a warning is given."

Emphatic Witness for God

Questions raised by the high tide at Long Beach and brought to mind with renewed force by information which the telescope furnished led me more fully to appreciate the strange power of attraction operating over and about us all the while. We have named it "gravity," but how little that means! Perhaps the secrets of atomic energy, now bursting from their age-old hiding, may help us much in learning what gravity is. But whether we learn that or not, we already know this tremendous energy well enough to be able to imagine somewhat accurately what an utter, overwhelming, devastating cataclysm would strike our universe were the reins called "gravity" suddenly to be removed.

Our sun may be thought of as the positive center (proton) of our system, and about it at tremendous speeds move the planets, moons, stars, and satellites, weaving in and out among one another, never varying their schedules by the fraction of a second. Even as the neutrons move about the positive core of the atom, so it may possibly be that the orbits of the heavenly bodies

87

lie about the central sun, all together forming our Solar System which we are told may be relatively small when compared with other similar aggregates of heavenly bodies. And all these systems are here, stretching out into a whole which no finite mind can conceive, and warning every rational being against the folly of ignoring what they reveal about their Creator and Operator.

The theories regarding the universe, its size, the relations of its various planetary systems, and such, seem so definitely to be established that they make some correlative hypotheses also appear to be inescapable facts. These are:

1. This vast, incomprehensible, interrelated series of heavenly bodies becomes more and more a baffling intellectual problem to anyone who refuses to believe that mind preceded matter; or stated conversely, to anyone who holds that matter or energy rather than mind is eternal. Now, when we can be pretty sure that matter is but a manifestation of energy, we are confronted more closely than ever before with Reason's demand for an explanation of the almost infinite number of manifestations which this energy takes. It would be easier to explain the tides to a benighted savage who never heard of gravitation's law and never saw the sea than to account for the wonderful order, harmony, and cohesiveness of Nature to one who does not know the God of Abraham and of Isaac, the Father of our Lord Jesus Christ!

2. When one considers the utilitarian nature of many things and adds to that the definite way in which rational beings not only appropriate such things but learn to improve them, he adds emphasis to the *a priori* argument for God. Reason can produce no adequate explanation of such phenomena unless the eternal, creative, rational Being whom we call God is accepted!

Looking at the tides reveals the working of a bit of the energy which operates among the various planetary bodies. Looking at Saturn and Mars through a strong telescope reveals more clearly the vast expanse by which they are separated from our minute planet. Finding in the atom the secret of all things which

88

we class as material uncovers more completely the mystery of origins and lets every honest student know that nothing short of absolute faith in the creation story of Genesis, emphasized and elaborated by Hebrews 11:3, makes sense or answers the inner demand of a free soul for certain truth.

Planets at Play

"One other lesson is easily drawn from the experiences under consideration," Father Time adds to the argument. "Just as the moon and wind produce a dangerous tide against which feeble man is helpless, even so the interplay of planets and Solar Systems is leading inevitably to some universal cataclysm which none can imagine, much less describe. Were man not so wholly engrossed by pleasure and so enslaved mentally by various hypotheses through which he finds temporary satisfaction for his hungry spirit, we might expect some change in attitude toward the Word of God. Consequently, we might expect a more concerted effort to discover just what scientific principles are involved in its prophecies regarding the end of this age and of our known world.

"'Conservation of Matter' is one hypothesis which it now seems will have to be displaced, and instead 'Conservation of Energy' must be set. The breaking of the atom into its component energy-elements seems pretty definitely to do away with the theory that matter loses none of its essential bulk and weight when changed from one form to another, as when coal burns. If one could convert a pound of coal into atomic energy, you may well demand, Would that energy weigh a pound either before or after being expended? Can one weigh energy? Is an electric wire heavier when carrying 40,000 volts of energy than when carrying 110 volts?

"God's Book declares that the elements, the component parts of heavenly bodies, will melt with fervent heat during the spectacular hour when time shall have ended (II Peter 3:5–10). Here is as accurate a scientific statement as anyone could now

89

make. Peter, moved by the Spirit of truth, put into a few Greek words an exact description of what will take place when the Power which holds atomic energy to its appointed task in the universe shall be withdrawn. Then, indeed, will your earth and other bodies disintegrate, and out of the original, primordial elements—protons and neutrons—God will form a new Heaven and a new earth!

"Does that sound fantastic and utterly impossible? Then try earnestly to imagine what you would have thought, had you been present when God the Father was holding counsel with the other members of the Trinity, Jesus Christ and the Holy Spirit, and probably with a host of angelic beings, and said, 'Let us make man,' or when He declared, 'Let there be light.' If your imagination is good, step back with Him to where there was nothing visible in a physical sense; only energy to feel the sway of the eternal mind of God. Would it have seemed any easier for the Creator to direct this infinite energy into such physical forms as you know than it will be for Him to return that energy to its original state and then reshape it? Which is simpler: for man to produce ice or to convert ice into water and that water into steam?

"A generation ago scientists sneered when preachers stressed the Biblical account of the end of this world and the spectacular conflagration which will come. Today, anomalous as it may seem, scientists are describing the catastrophic end of our planet when atomic energy will actually set it on fire and burn it up; and many preachers, wise in their own conceits, are sneering at the men of science! The elements will melt with fervent heat! Of that all men need to be sure. Even if preacher or scientist or both reject that prophecy, the march of time toward that inevitable day of the Lord cannot be stayed.

"Science has done nothing during this century more definite than its production of data which support the Bible account of judgment which is being held in store for this earth and its ungodly people. There is coming a time when 'the trump of God shall sound' and time shall cease! When that day arrives, the restraining bonds will suddenly be loosed, and wild, utter chaos will again exist where now we have order. The physical universe will disintegrate midst heat and noise which are unthinkable by our finite minds. Chaos will once more exist where the cosmos has been so long.

"The rip tide is gathering itself under cover while foolish human beings go about the business of having a good time. God's lifeguards in many places are sounding the warning, 'The end draweth nigh. Prepare to meet thy God!' (Amos 4:11–13). But 'as the days of Noah were, so shall also the coming of the Son of Man be' (Matt. 24:37–39). The masses not only do not heed the lifeguards, but turn spitefully upon every one of them who dares condemn sin, denounce the sensuous pleasures of the day. He who seeks to direct any organized movement to shackle the sordid hands of those who, for the sake of money to be made, are abetting the complete prostitution of the human family is a marked man. Instead of being warned, the masses, including many church members, are turning, as the prophet foretold they would do in the latter days, to teachers whose ears itch for compliments (II Tim. 4:3), who smile at sin, and take part in what they call innocent pastime!"

Suddenly Time's sermon ended, and I was afraid! Then from within a voice seemed to cry, "What a time for the John the Baptists to be out with their warning shouts, 'Repent, for the day of judgment is at hand!' What a day for men like Peter, the Hermit, to preach a crusade against the infidels who help increase human degeneracy, and to enlist hosts of virile young people to fight for God and right! What a time for the followers of Christ to be pleading for mercy and grace! 'Tis the day when Christians should be aroused by the growing din and clamor which sin is turning loose about them, when the hosts should be getting ready so that when Christ comes, a militant, happy band may be waiting. A people ready to receive Him because working all the while with might and main to prepare for His com-

91

ing." Let us, therefore, turn the "Battle Hymn of the Republic" into

A CHANT OF CHALLENGE

Oh, look and know the surety of the coming of
 the Lord!
Hear Him calling through the prophets,
 "Heed the warnings of my Word!"
He has loosed the fateful atom,
  Which will prove a mighty sword,
   Our God is moving on!

What a challenge He now issues
  To believers everywhere!
'Tis enough to send them trooping
  Down to every house of prayer!
Time grows shorter! End approaches!
  Let humanity beware,
   For God is hast'ning on.

Like humanity in weakness
  Christ was born across the sea
Came in human flesh to save us,
  From the curse of sin to free
All who heed His invitation,
  Who with hearts aglow can see
   His day now drawing nigh.

Oh, hear ye, Christians, hear ye
  God's great challenge for your day!
Turn from pleasures, sin and evil!
  Serve your Master while you may!
Time is fleeting, Christ approaches
  For His final judgment day,
   While time goes marching on.

CHAPTER SEVEN

Pike's Peak, a Pulpit

On to the Top!

I simply will not go any farther; this cold is freezing me, and I can hardly breathe!"

"But, Lady, you don't want to stay here all alone for twelve hours, do you?"

"I'd rather remain here alone that long than be in a grave by myself longer," came the sharp retort.

The brief dialogue took place one morning at the Halfway Camp up the side of Pike's Peak. A party of schoolteachers, on their way home from Educational Week at the San Francisco World's Fair, were climbing the mountain to see the sunrise. They were making the trip on the backs of plodding burros and had been resting for some time at the camp near the timber line. Shortly after midnight the guide had aroused those who had been fortunate enough to drop off to sleep. It was time to resume the climb.

One lady, who had been quite nauseated during the previous evening after we entered the rarefied atmosphere, was feeling unusually miserable and did not want to go on. The guide was afraid to leave her unattended in that lonely spot, and none of

Looking to the Hills

Through tall, rock-crested hills I hear
The Psalmist's voice ring rich and clear,
"Lift up your eyes! Let heart draw near
The Rock that banishes all fear!"

The mountains grand—each rugged hill—
Reveal to man what God's good will
Doth offer all who trust Him, till
His holy purpose He fulfill.

Assurance comes from each bold peak
That God will care for all the weak.
Encouragement, the hills bespeak
For all who peace and comfort seek.

Then trust His power! Whate'er He say
Believe! When He doth show the way,
Securely led, our spirits may
Look calmly toward each dawning day.

the party was willing to forego the pleasure of the trip even to play the part of a Good Samaritan.

The matter was adjusted after a time. Meanwhile, we were being mounted on sturdy little beasts, wrapped in blankets and slickers, provided with heavy fleece-lined gloves, and our feet securely encased in warm covers. Soon we were off, strung out behind the lead guide, on our way to the summit of the famous mountain.

By three o'clock in the morning we had reached the Summit House and were soon inside, seeking warmth. A snowstorm the previous afternoon had spread a blanket on the sheltered parts of the peak, and the cold which it brought with it was quite intense. A bitter wind was whistling across the vast unbroken spaces to the northwest. It struck the mountaintop without hindrance, seeming bent on moving what man had dared erect in its path, or at least on showing man how futile are his efforts at resisting Nature.

Not long could I endure the inside of the house. The discomfort of the hot, rare air and the fumes of cooking, mingled with the inevitable tobacco smoke, soon led me to prefer the biting cold outside. I went out on the terrace, found a corner where I was somewhat sheltered from the wind, and waited for Old Sol to poke his fiery crown from below the distant horizon.

All around me were patches of snow, marking with whiteness the nooks among the ragged stones which were piled layer on layer in wild profusion for the last half-mile up the mountain. I knew the sun would soon be rising, and I knew that the colors would be most beautiful before it had topped the distant timber line. The storm of the previous afternoon had washed the air clean and made way for a spectacular sunrise. The guide had congratulated the party heartily upon being fortunate enough to visit the peak on just that occasion.

It is impossible to describe such a sunrise as that provided the morning of August 15, 1915! The scene I saw there that day was enough to pay me many times over for the hardships I endured in making the climb on burro-back. The exquisitely shaded colors that slowly adorned the mists and the scattered clouds in the East constituted an artist's loveliest canvas. The soft feathery spangles of daintily tinted clouds trailing off across the sky were as beautiful as an angel's dream. High above me the green-blue sky slowly turned to rose, while toward the West, lavender and lilac gradually covered the larger clouds whose edges were etched with burnished silver, trimmed with old gold lace.

Away below, two miles and more under the Summit House, lay the wide world, still black and dour under the somber shades of night. It was too early, I knew, for the cocks to be crowing in the distance. Cows were still sleeping quietly. I well could imagine the restfulness of the surroundings of many a farm-house, as I looked upon the distant fields, barely discernible through shrouds of darkness and mist.

Slowly but steadily the light made its way downward until the valley below was touched and one could clearly see fields and farm buildings. With only the natural sight to depend upon, one had the impression that he was gazing upon the bed of some giant, for the regular pattern of pastures and fields of ripening grain looked like a vast patchwork quilt, and the rolling land readily lent itself to the impression of some giant form asleep under the cover. The threads of green meandering across the plain marked the courses of streams. Here and there one could just make out a line along which an occasional automobile passed, looking, from our post, like a mite crawling along a white lisle thread.

As I stood there that morning, a bit apart from others of the party who came out when the guide called them, I somehow was reminded of Zacchaeus and his experience one day in Jericho when the Son of Man was passing through. My mind imagined a contrast between my experience and his. I had climbed the rugged hillside in the face of the increasing cold and the grow-ing perils of falling. He had gone to the treetop in the face of cold unconcern on the part of his friends and neighbors, against their opposition, in spite of their jeers. He had climbed, not into a biting cold wind as I had done, but in the face of cruel friendlessness. I had climbed to see a spectacular manifestation of divine power; he had climbed to see the Author of divine power. I stood rejoicing because of the mighty natural spectacle; he raced down from the tree, rejoicing over being addressed by Jesus of Nazareth. I went home taking a mental picture which yet remains vivid; Zacchaeus went home taking with him the Son of God who, before the evening had passed, had become his very own Redeemer!

Nearly forty years have gone since that eventful occasion on Pike's Peak. During those years Father Time has had opportunity to present vital lessons which the incidents connected with that interesting climb brought to my attention. Now, as I think of these things, I seem to see him, standing atop Pike's Peak—a pulpit of the ages—and hear him speak with clear, commanding, resonant voice to my soul:

"Child of Nature, would you know the truth and have your spirit freed by it to climb to where you can see realities of eternal moment? Would you get above the ordinary affairs of life, such as eating and drinking, gratifying carnal desires for a season, struggling for things that do not satisfy? Would you realize the goal for which rational beings were made? Would you know why the eternal God created man in His own image, thereby making it inevitable that he should have his own way, choose his own roads, decide upon his own goals and determine his own eternal destiny? Then bear with me a while, and I will point out to you some significant lessons.

Seeing and Knowing

"The testimony of others about any person, place, or thing can never satisfy a normal human being. Curiosity, the hunger of a rational being for knowledge, may be whetted by what another says, but it cannot be satisfied. As a child cannot be

97

content with a parent's description of some new gadget, even so has the Creator decreed that the adult should always desire to know more than can be learned from the words of other people.

"You had heard of Pike's Peak; you had read about it; you listened eagerly when others told of visits to the mountain. You had read about Mt. Mitchell, Mammoth Cave in Kentucky, and Mammouth Springs in Arkansas. You studied while yet in grammar school about the Washington Monument, a picture of which graced a page of your textbook. You had read about and seen pictures of the Eiffel Tower in Paris and Westminster Abbey in London. You had sung 'London Bridge Is Falling Down' multiplied times, knowing all the while that it would not fall. You had heard and read much about Niagara Falls, the Royal Gorge, Golden Gate, Great Salt Lake, the Cliffs of Dover, the Jungfrau, and other scenic wonders. But only vague ideas could ever be formed by your mind regarding them. If you had never seen them yourself, how much poorer you would be! One must secure firsthand information, if he would know the fuller, richer, more satisfying experience of living.

"It is even so with the Prince of Peace whom Zacchaeus sought to see that day in Jericho. The preaching of the best ministers and the words of the finest teachers can do no more than arouse one's interest in Him and inspire in one a determination to see Him. Countless essays, poems, hymns, and psalms written in His praise are inadequate vessels with which to convey to other minds a true picture of Him. The Holy Law is a schoolmaster, a pedagogue, whose business it is to see that you reach the feet of the Teacher; but it can do no more than direct your steps to Him. The Gospel is the testimony of the ages, condensed by the Holy Spirit of God for your benefit; but it is only the instrument whereby you are led or driven to the Source of salvation and security. Let all these agencies serve to arouse your interest in things that are above, and direct you to Him who is the Way, the Truth, and the Life; then, like the noted publican of that ancient Hebrew city, you will soon be climbing over selfishness, sin, worldliness, and desire for personal ease and pleasure, because you have become convinced that there is no price too great to stand between your immortal soul and the Saviour.

"It is as impossible rightly to evaluate Jesus of Nazareth by reading what others have said about Him as it is to know the glories of nature from descriptions given you by immature minds. Only when you have gone to the Mount and heard Him preach; when you have heard His imperial commands to wind and sea, to devils and Death; when you have scaled Golgotha and watched Him die midst the shudders and rumblings caused by Nature's revulsion at His death; when you have stood beside that empty tomb and heard His messenger shout, 'He is not here, for He is risen!'; when you have walked up Olivet's slope and watched Him pass in a spectacular burst of glory; and when you have waited to hear an angel assure you, 'This same Jesus, which is taken up from you into heaven, shall so come in like manner as ye have seen him go into heaven' (Acts 1:11)—only then can you know Him as Lord and God. You should never forget that until He is thus known, any rational being is poor indeed and greatly to be pitied. Do your best, therefore, to lead men everywhere to know Him through personal, intimate contacts which everyone may have with Him. Death's sickle will remain sharp and sure until man accepts Him who holds in His hands the keys of death!

The Hard Way Best

"Another lesson you need to know, my son, is one embodied long ago in an adage: 'There is no royal road to success.' Whoever expects to attain heights from which things may be seen in their broadest aspects, from which one may discover the interrelationships which constitute such a vital part of all reality, must be willing to pay a steep price. The richest beauty of sunrise or sunset can never be witnessed by people too indolent to scale a mountain or too timid to go aloft in a plane. The glory of a great forest with the myriad fascinating things which it holds will never be enjoyed by one who is unwilling to carry tired feet and to suffer bruises and scratches secured while tramping where car and even cart never made track. If you want to be big of soul and have that within your own grasp which makes life full and your spirit buoyant and powerful, then know that you must pay the price demanded by the laws of God.

"Suppose you had been willing to stay at the Halfway House on Pike's Peak! Your already tired muscles bade you do so. Already the chafing of saddle leather had made thighs and calves sore. The brief nap at the Halfway House and the fire in the rarefied air produced extreme lassitude. The bright glow and the warmth of the fire were far more alluring than the cold, raw air and the mounting piles of boulders up and up into the shadows of night. You had not gone to Manitou and Colorado Springs, however, merely to visit the lowlands and see timber and springs; you had gone to scale Pike's Peak, to get much nearer to the skies than you had ever been before.

"He who takes the easy way in life can never hope to enjoy the richest things which Nature has for her children. Things grown in a hothouse may be beautiful to the eye, but they cannot be as stable or as fragrant as things that struggle up in fields and woods. People who choose the easy way in life are doomed to miss both the thrill of overcoming serious obstacles and the richer, fuller joy of personal achievement. The boy who depends upon his parents to do his arithmetic; who relies upon Dad for all his playthings; who never ventures out upon his own, will hardly grow into a leader of men, a creator of new things. The girl who lies abed while her mother cooks breakfast, does dishes, and cleans house; who depends upon the merchants to provide her every dress; who never has made a mud pie, a doll dress or a playhouse, will, in all probability, eventually lose interest in life and slowly stifle the love and respect of her husband.

"The farmer who refuses to work when it is wet or cold; who lies abed late merely because yesterday's work was hard, will soon be living in a ramshackle house and tilling depleted soil with dilapidated equipment. The merchant, the professional man, especially a preacher, the baker, the candlestick maker, the banker, the industrialist—anyone who succeeds does so because he is not afraid of hard work. You will hear hosts of people bemoaning their 'hard luck,' or berating more fortunate people for holding them back and refusing them a chance; but, if you will investigate, you will usually find that they have been held back not by others but by their own unwillingness to endure hardships.

"The party chose the hard way of scaling Pike's Peak; temporarily you suffered physical discomfort and bodily pain. When you reached the starting point some twenty hours after having set forth on the climb, some could hardly walk, so sore and strained had their muscles become. But when you left Denver the following day and compared notes with other tourists who were on the train, you discovered how valuable your bruises were. After calling attention to one scene after another which they who rode upon the cog train did not enjoy, you could pat your sore thighs and be glad for them.

"So is it all the way through life. One grows tired of studies and refuses to finish high school; another refuses to go to college. Some youths become enamored of the pleasures of the day and are out at night indulging the flesh. Others look beyond today with its allurements and, seeing the distant hills with their bluecrowned peaks, are set to forget the things at hand except as they may be made steppingstones to worthy things in the future. Worn, frayed clothes are used if need be instead of new silks and serges. Wholesome food is taken at all times instead of knickknacks. Long, gruelling hours of study and toil are chosen instead of the ease and comforts which the social-minded covet and seek. Eventually, inevitably, youth passes by, middle age comes and goes, and suddenly each one who has survived approaches old age with its increasing helplessness and growing longing for the end of the road.

"Where then are the things that seemed so attractive and alluring to youth? What has become of the nights of reveling and their subsequent daylight hours of rest? They have been turned over to a new generation of foolish folk who will not learn from me how to estimate the cost of accepting them. Where are the things that are solid, dependable, durable? Not in the places of commercialized amusements! Not down at the dance hall, tavern, theater, or night spot! They are held by people who, like Hercules of Grecian folklore, chose the path of labor—who had vision enough while young to see that one's life is made full, rich, and enduring by toils and tears, by struggles and sorrows, by self-abnegation and suffering which must be encountered from childhood to full maturity by everyone who aspires to climb to any worthwhile height of achievement."

Climbing and Visions

Another fine lesson was learned from the experiences at Pike's Peak, and it may be summed up in one sentence: "Whoever expects to become a good director of man's earthly destiny must strive until he has risen above the plains upon which the masses move."

"Will you turn," Father Time now seems to say, "to the famous words about Moses, 'He endured as seeing him who is invisible' (Heb. 11:27), and think on that saying with me? There is no more heroic incident on record than that of Moses' turning his back upon the riches of Egypt, upon a throne which carried with it pomp and temporal power and everything which wealth, power, immediate fame, and vast stores of choice worldly goods, 'choosing rather to suffer afflictions with the people of God than to enjoy the pleasures of sin for a season' (Heb. 11:25). What made him take the step?

"It was the vision of an enslaved race which he might help liberate. It was the call of blood, answering a cry of distress which reached his ears from the slave pens below him. He had scaled the heights by study in the schools of Egypt. He had broadened his vision of human need by comparing his own luxurious surroundings with the wretched state of the despised Hebrews. Through lessons learned while he was yet under the care of his mother-nurse, from things which had been conveyed to him by the wise men of his own race, and through impulses which were aroused within him by the Spirit of God, he had developed until he was able to distinguish the real from the artificial, the actual from the fictitious. In other words, Moses had become a constructive force in human affairs of his day.

"One is never impelled to venture forth upon dangerous enterprises until his spiritual eyes have been opened wide enough to see not only the immediate price to be paid but the ultimate prize to be gained. And he will not have such a vision unless he rises above the purely carnal and secular. It is the call of the invisible which makes one willing to be venturesome, sacrificial, heroic; and that call never comes to one who lives on the low plane; it is heard in its most challenging tones by the few who pay the price of climbing up to where they view the whole arena of life and of learning how to direct some of the players so they may win the game.

The Way Beyond

"What shall the future hold in store for the human family?" Father Time queried. "Is there nothing for man to look forward to except the endless conflict which grows out of selfishness and its inordinate lust for wealth and power? Will each succeeding generation of civilized people go on building according to faulty human plans, only to have their children wreck the structures before the builders have all died? You have seen far-flung vistas where nothing remains of what once was beautiful and productive. You have also viewed large areas that today are far more attractive and fruitful than they were a generation or more ago. What makes the difference? There is but one answer: different men produce opposite effects by their lives and labors. One section of society constructs a Tower of Babel; another rids Nature's fields of rubbish, makes them productive and thus lays the foundation for a great nation!

"You have seen one community wherein dwelt happy people in neat, comfortable homes, surrounded by evidences of thrift and rarely disturbed by any form of lawlessness. Residences, schools, churches, business enterprises, parks, and playgrounds told of peace, plenty, and neighborly kindness. Few police ever patrolled that area. On the other hand, you have been in sections where everything was run-down and dilapidated. The houses were shacks; the streets were littered with rubbish; people were dirty and listless; no church spires pointed upward to something worth seeking. The school buildings were sorry, unattractive structures which seemed to glower at the underprivileged waifs who tramped toward them. Police officers, though numerous, could not keep down violence and crime. What makes the dierence between such communities? Again there can be but one answer: it is made by people.

"Now, here is what all human beings need to have fixed in their minds so securely they shall never forget it. *People are what they are largely because of whom they follow and what they seek.* As long, therefore, as any community lacks the right leadership, its people will live on a low level; and as long as they have no higher motive for living than to gratify the desires of the flesh, they will continue to be a drag about the feet of any social body to which they are attached. The crying need of any generation is to be led by people who have had courage and hardihood enough to resist the demands of the flesh, to overcome the handicaps which it always puts about human spirits, and to climb high enough above the common plane to be able to see and know how to incite the masses to try to break loose from restraining bonds, to conquer lethargy, and to fight nobly to attain a higher level than that which holds them, whatever it may be.

"More than a century ago Charles Dickens found himself living midst a political and economic mess which was threaten-

104

ing to bring disaster to England. The invention of the power loom and of other labor-saving machinery had thrown loose in Europe, and especially in England, a mass of unemployed laborers. Riots, sabotage, bloodshed, pillage and even murder increased, and civil war was imminent. Prisons were overrun with debtors, and poverty stretched her gaunt hands farther and farther as the empty days came and went. Dickens had risen to where he could see both the pitiable plight of the unemployed and the dangerous state of their former employers. He spared neither the one group nor the other, but in a series of stories and essays held the whole sorry social scheme up to ridicule, at the same time presenting plans for readjustments both in mental attitudes and in industrial and social relationships. He was derided by many; he was praised by some; he was hated by the greedy sinners who would jeopardize all rather than lose some of their fat profits. But Dickens' vision and message helped to save the nation for her mighty place in affairs of a later day.

"There are two alternatives before you and others who live with you: You may sit idly by until social and moral conditions have degenerated to where such controls as honor, honesty, kindness, love, fair dealing and social justice have been destroyed. How rapidly this is being done may be seen by anyone who will look about him. Who now cares what others think about him? Whose word will the public accept today as good as his bond? What evidence of brotherly kindness is there in the sordid and mad rush wherein each seeks his own, and masses of men sell their liberty to overlords who promise them the largest immediate financial returns? What is happening to love in a world where the sacred holy tie of marriage is derided in every issue of the secular press; where fiction belittles the sacredness of marriage and glorifies illicit sex relations; where children are led in school, at movies, and on playgrounds to rebel against the parent who seeks to control and direct? What happens to fair play where young people are taught that survival of the fittest is nature's law, hence that they are wise who by cunning and cold-blooded activity command the stage? How long can justice survive in a country where legal sanctions are flouted and decisions of judges, all the way from the umpire of a sandlot ball game to justices of the Supreme Court of your nation, are prone to be determined not by law but by pressure groups, even by bribes? Does common sense lead one to ignore these and other indications of approaching social catastrophe?

"The other alternative is to face the issues and set up a movement which will not only challenge the degrading forces but will instill into the hearts of the populace so much of the idealism of Jesus Christ that soon a big majority will rise in rebellion against selfishness, entrenched evil, and antisocial forces of every other kind and put an end to the system that exalts the low, vulgar, profane, and licentious. Whoever has been lifted up high enough to survey the future in the light of the past should immediately see that this must be done soon, that it is now a social, political, and moral imperative.

"The future holds an orderly government based upon the principles of Christianity or it holds a system of human slavery which must inevitably come, unless men can be made to appreciate personal liberty and be willing to pay the price which liberty demands for her services. There must be a government, national and international, based upon the ethics of Jesus, or inevitably there will be a reign by selfish overlords whose hearts will know no pity, whose minds will recognize no claim but their own wishes, and whose haughty spirits will gloat over the sufferings, miseries and even deaths of those who have forfeited freedom to them.

"The future holds in store whatever the youth of today may be led to espouse with the heart. If they continue to yield their bodies as servants of sin, to be dominated by carnal desires, and to squander their physical, mental, and moral substance in wild, riotous living, what can come tomorrow except ruin? If they continue to allow themselves to be carried into the maelstrom of low thinking produced by sensuous pictures, literature, loose

106

conduct and corrupt, profane speech, then they will doom themselves, their country, and their offspring to ignominy, ruin and destruction.

"On the other hand, if you and others, because older and wiser, can somehow bring your talents into fullest play and use all your powers in a great, enthusiastic, daring effort to lead hosts of young people to the knowledge there is something ahead worth climbing for, something to do worth preparing for, something to gain worth risking death to achieve, there is hope, glorious hope, of turning the tides. You who have seen sunrise from Pike's Peak, who have heard the thunder of Niagara from the Cave of the Winds, who have felt the thrilling experiences of achievement won at the cost of personal ease and temporal pleasure; you who have caught a vision must hold before the youth and middle-aged people of today the idealism of Jesus Christ. Point out to them in clear, unambiguous terms the certain impending tragedies which will meet them if they continue to run afoul of the laws of God.

"Having drawn for them the contrast between the fruits of the flesh and those of noble spirits, challenge them one and all to turn from ease and temporal pleasure for the sake of preparing to defend the unthinking masses in their inalienable right to life, liberty, and the pursuit of happiness. Show them what it will mean to the world of tomorrow if they will fight and sacrifice and persist to the end that the teachings of the New Testament may be made the basis upon which the social and political structures of the coming days may rest.

"Moses never had a finer opportunity of gaining immortal fame by championing the rights of the enslaved Hebrews of his day than our youth now have, if only they will challenge the low, sordid, selfish, money-mad men and women who, for the sake of easily-earned riches, are damning a nation by polluting its children and young people. John the Baptist had no more glorious privilege when he paved the way for the coming of the new King than daring, inspired souls now have if they will open the way for a return of sane, simple, sacrificial living on earth and in our own America.

"The day is far spent; the shadows of night already are thickening in the valleys. Laborers are weary; many are growing faint and would stop at rest camps before the end of the trail is reached. Go, my son! Go and lead others to join in a grim battle to the end that the visions of the few prophetic saints of your day may determine the dreams others will enjoy when their life's span approaches its end and their sun draws near its western horizon!"

That sermon ended. Father Time seemed to close his Book before my eyes. Suddenly he was gone and Pike's Peak melted away! I sat alone with my paper and pen. "What now shall I write?" I asked, and from the halls of memory there came a voice bidding me add a paraphrase of Joaquin Miller's "Columbus," written during April, 1925, to enhearten Belmont Heights Baptist Church of Nashville, Tennessee, faltering before a building enterprise which to many of them and their friends seemed entirely beyond their reach. With some adaptations that bit of verse is added here with an earnest desire that all who read it may heed the challenge and get desperately busy about the business of the Master whose everlasting command to His followers is, "Be thou faithful unto death, and I will give you a crown of life" (Rev. 2:10).

PRESS ON AND ON!

Behind us lies a deep, dark stream;
Behind a road both long and drear;
Before us not the faintest gleam
Of hope, our doleful hearts to cheer.
Some men exclaim, "Now let us pray,
For light and cheer are both full-gone."
But Master, speak! What shall we say?
Why say, "Press on! Press on and on!"

We grow more anxious, each and all.
Strong men grow fearful, tired and worn,
And stout hearts think of ease. A pall
Of dark gloom comes, depressing and forlorn.
What shall we say, dear Master, say,
If we see naught but struggle at the dawn?
Why, you shall say at dawn each day,
"Press on! Press on! Press on and on!"

We trudge and toil while troubles grow
Until at last the weak complain,
"Why, even God cannot now show
How this great goal we may attain."
Our only hope seems passed away,
And faith from many hearts is gone.
Now speak, dear Master, speak and say!
He cries, "Press on! Press on and on!"

We stand aghast! Then comes the cry,
"We're tired and worn and sick of fight!"
Some make complaints while others lie
With ready feet as if for flight.
Dear Master, speak! In mercy's name
What shall we do when hope is gone?
His words leap back, aglow, aflame!
"Press on! Press on! Press on and on!"

Dear God, we hear! We'll press our way
And work, though hardships sore and hard
May beat us down; for there's a day
When toil and travail have reward.
A joyous shout will come, "Hurrah!
A new day's sun doth rise! We've won!"
We'll reach the heights! We'll let all learn
God's glorious lesson, "On! Press on!"

HE SITS AND THINKS

CHAPTER EIGHT

Silver King at Last

Learning to Fish

DON'T PULL YOUR POLE so soon, and don't jerk so hard when you do pull!"

The admonition was by a man to his eight-year-old son who sat beside him on the bank of Little River. It was the lad's first fishing experience, and his eagerness and excitement caused him to give his pole a quick, vigorous jerk every time his cork began to dance on the water. "Wait until the cork goes well under and then give an easy jerk and pull steadily," continued the wise one.

The boy tried earnestly to obey the instructions. Fish were hungry and he had plenty of strikes. Slowly but steadily he overcame the tendency to pull his line too soon and learned instead how to set his hook and then hold a steady line while drawing his catch to the shore or lifting it out of the water.

During many succeeding fishing trips he learned not only how to handle his tackle, but not to become disheartened because fish did not bite often enough and not to lose his head and "blow off" when a good fish got off his hook before being landed. He overcame the tendency to be exasperated, even

111

angry, when only worthless fish would bite, or when minnows repeatedly robbed his hook. A day spent where he knew fish lived came to be a pleasant day, even if he made no catch. He discovered that persistence in angling never fails to bring its reward. He learned that no fish caught, however worthless it may be, is a total loss to the angler, since hooking it brings a certain pleasure in anticipating what it may be. Then, too, landing it contributes definite improvement in the technique of angling.

When a large adolescent boy, he went with his father to Anderson's Ferry where they secured an old skiff and, dropping down several hundred yards, anchored to the projecting limb of an oak tree which months before had fallen into the stream.

"This is a likely looking place," the man said when the boat was securely tied. "Be as quiet as possible, for water carries every sound in the boat, and good fish are easily frightened."

They were using long, slender cane poles with plenty of spare line. This enabled them to reach out some distance in any direction, and made it easier to prevent a fish, once it had been hung, from running under some obstruction with the line. With a frisky shiner on each hook, they set to work to entice the "big boy" who, they felt sure, was lurking in the blue-green waters.

Diligently they plied their poles, shifting the bait from one place to another and keeping it moving in the water between shifts. But the corks were undisturbed by anything stronger than the bait. After more than an hour they decided it was not the right time for bass, so shifted to worms and tried for perch and bream. Their luck was only a little better; they caught four small sun perch and one goggle-eye. A big school of minnows came along, and the worms quickly disappeared among them. After another hour had dragged by, the boy pulled in his hook, baited it anew with a minnow, cast the bait into an unobstructed pool, and laid down his pole.

"It isn't time to quit, Son," his father said, smiling.

112

"I know it," replied the boy, "but there's no use in holding out a pole when nothing will bite."

"How do you know they won't bite?" asked the man. "If you don't offer them a bait, you can't know whether they will bite or not."

"Well, haven't I been offering them a bait—two kinds of bait? I've done nothing else for three hours."

"But that doesn't prove that they won't bite," insisted his dad. "You don't stay hungry all the time, do you? And when you are not hungry, you don't go to the trouble of hunting for food. It's when you are really hungry that you grab for a bite to eat. Fish are like that. The big difference lies in the fact that you have a habit of eating at certain times each day, while fish know nothing about clocks. They eat when they are hungry, and it's a fisherman's business to see that the feed is on hand when they are in the notion of taking it. Whoever grows tired or gets disheartened and quits will have few fish on his table."

"I guess you're right," the boy admitted, "but it's no fun fishing if they don't bite."

"That's what you think," his father replied, "but you are dead wrong. Imagine how much fun it will be when one does strike! You know that the longer you wait for a piece of good pie or a dish of ice cream the better it tastes when you get it. Likewise, the longer you wait to hang a game fish the bigger the thrill it will give you—watch your line! You've got a strike!"

The lad glanced to where his cork had been, and it was out of sight. He quickly caught up his pole, gave it a firm jerk, and almost shouted when he felt his line hold against something bulky; he did shout when the fish began to run and then suddenly jumped clear of the water. It was a big-mouth bass weighing, he felt sure, more than five pounds.

"Steady, Son!" cautioned his father when the excited boy began to pull too hard on the struggling fish. "Take your time and enjoy the sport."

The lad did. The long, slender, cane pole and the extra yards of line enabled him to play with the fish. He had much ado to prevent its making a too sudden lurch against a taut line, or running under a submerged limb of the fallen tree. Four times the fellow jumped out of the water, his big mouth wide open as he sought to dislodge the hook. With eager hope and racing heart the young angler played his catch until finally it was tired and could be drawn near enough to be lifted into the skiff.

"Now who wanted to quit?" his father asked when the fish was in hand and was being "hefted" to estimate its weight.

"I'll not be ready again to quit just because I don't get a bite," replied the boy. "I'd fish a whole week just to catch another like this."

"And you'll probably fish many a week before catching another like that," replied his dad.

Where Tarpon Play

The years went by. The boy became a mature man who more and more enjoyed the sport of angling. But always, even when he had had a good catch, there was a sense of frustration in his heart, for he wanted to catch a larger fish than fresh water afforded. Pictures and stories in sportsmen's magazines told him about the larger fish which live in the sea; his ambition as an angler kept before him all along the idea of landing some day a big game fish from salt water. And at last he reached the place where he had a chance to realize his long-cherished hope.

"Just hold a close line and be on your toes every second. If you get a strike and do not instantly set your hook, it will be too late, for a tarpon doesn't tarry after he strikes your bait."

This advice the angler heard one May evening while a party of fishermen was being taken to the outlet of Tampa Bay, Florida. He listened eagerly to every word from the skipper who was an old hand at salt-water fishing. Tarpon were plentiful and had been running in goodly numbers with each incoming tide. Only one of the party, in addition to the skipper, had ever caught a tarpon; only three had ever done any sea fishing. The counsel was, therefore, very timely, and among all who heard it none considered it more seriously than did the ambitious angler from Arkansas.

The party pushed across the bay and just at dusk anchored at a point where the incoming tide ran swiftly. Soon five lines had been rigged up with heavy hooks and big floats which would break loose should a fish be hung. Each line was carried on a big, automatic reel which would loosen the line against a winding crank when a fish exerted more than a maximum strain on it. A perch-like live bait weighing a pound or more was attached to each hook thrown over the side of the boat and allowed to drift some hundred yards with the running tide. Once again the skipper cautioned the men to keep on the alert every moment so as to sink the hook the instant a big fish struck.

The great struggle which goes on endlessly in the sea was in evidence, for the tarpon churned the waters not far from the boat. By the light of a nearly full moon one could see the swirl made when a silver king came near the surface in its rush for a speeding victim. Eager eyes watched the nearby waters; tense left hands held the heavy rods and ready right hands clutched the reel cranks, set for instantaneous action. Darkness deepened. The moonbeams danced across the small whitecaps or upon the spray made by a striking fish.

"Look out!" suddenly yelled the skipper, slapping one fisherman on the shoulder. Up came the rod, but the tarpon had gone on, taking the bait with it. "You can't wait a split second on them fellers!" admonished the skipper. "The minute your line jerks, give it all you've got!"

The hook was rebaited, a float attached to the line and the sport continued. A few moments later I got my first strike, but I, too, was a bit tardy and had to draw in an empty hook. When my hook was rebaited and the float was again running back behind the boat, I braced myself in my seat, reset the handle of my rod, took a new hold and determined that the next fish would not outwit me. All about us the game fellows were having a picnic among a school of small fish. Now and then a tarpon jumped out of the water in its rush after prey.

Then it happened! My line suddenly went taut and I instantly gave it as hard a yank as I could. The hook went home and held! I had roped a yearling steer in other days and knew what it meant to try to hold the "critter," but I never dreamed there was a fish that could pull as hard as a yearling! None but a fisherman can appreciate the setting or understand what happened during the minutes that followed.

When the tarpon realized that he was hung, he dashed for deeper waters. The float was washed loose. At a word from the skipper all other lines were reeled in. I sat spellbound, winding desperately at the reel but hearing it sing as the fish rushed off. Fifty yards or so the game fellow sped, then leaped high into the air, giving his head an angry shake as he did so. A strong pull on the line turned him in midair, and he hit the water full-length and dived for the bottom. Again the line raced behind him and the reel sang against the stiff clutch and my vigorous winding. A second, a third, a fifth time the silver king leaped madly from the water, his scales reflecting the moonbeams each time! But the hook held!

Fifteen minutes or so went by; I began to tire; the tarpon also weakened, and again I began to reel in the line. When he was only a few feet away, I was becoming quite sure of my prize and had somewhat relaxed. Then the line drew the big fellow to the surface not more than ten feet from the boat. The sight of the boat and the men on it must have struck terror to the tarpon, for once again he sprang clear of the water, almost close enough to splatter us when he shook himself in that last desperate effort to throw the hook. Fortunately, I had not relaxed my hold on the rod, so succeeded in holding a stiff line.

The tarpon hit the water head first, dived, and once more the reel sang as the desperate fish rushed away. The struggle was near its end, however. Again the drag of a dead load on the line answered the turning reel. No more did the king rebel against captivity. At last he was near enough for the gaff to hook his gill cover, and in a moment he lay full-length upon the deck, sixty-five pounds of spent energy! I had risen from my seat while he was being drawn on deck. When I saw him lying in the moonlight I knew that at last I had had an angler's highest privilege.

THE ANGLER

He sits and thinks while moments fly
And clouds go scudding 'cross the sky.
He seldom moves; intent is he
Upon the things he knows to be
Beneath the waters there close by.

He waits and broods. Sometimes a smile
Lights up his face. Perhaps a pile
Of flotsam brings his head about
And turns his thoughts from lusty trout
Which he with lures has sought the while.

Do fish not strike? Well, what cares he?
Another day is sure to be.
Another sun he knows will rise
With promise that he'll get the prize
Which every angler longs to see.

What if mosquitoes sing and bite,
And fishes never come in sight?
He's still content—the peaceful fool—
Since he's dead sure that from some pool
A "whale" will rise to bring delight.

Just give to him a holiday
When he with kit can go his way
To fishing grounds, and there alone,
With business cares and such all gone,
He'll spend a happy, helpful day.

The Master of men once called some fishermen to attend His school, and the invitation included the promise, "I will make you fishers of men" (Matt. 4:19). What did He imply thereby? What may any ambitious soul learn from a skilled fisherman that will greatly enhance his chances of success in life? As long as man has peopled the earth he has been producing fishers, so Time can bring up a vast array of witnesses to some truths that every rational being should heed.

A Good Seeker

"One important lesson which every good fisher learns is to be a good seeker," Father Time declares. "He can never know just where the fish may be feeding. Today the bass are playing among the brush and roots near the banks; tomorrow they may be out in deep pools. Today the bluefish may be running under the pier, ready to strike at almost any kind of bait; tomorrow they may be found only outside the breakers. Today only "hard heads" (saltwater catfish) and crabs may be biting; tomorrow a twenty-pound drum may thrill your heart! This June the schools of mackerel may run close inshore; next June one may find them only where the lazy swells are running and occasional whitecaps fleck the bosom of the deep. The important fact is: somewhere in stream or pond, in lake or sea, there are fish worth catching. If one fails today, he will strive all the harder the next time, knowing that sooner or later he will find them.

"How like striving for success in any calling that is! For every rational being there is a place and a task which carry success. Some people are content when once they have reached the shallows and found the fingerlings and dwarfs. Others press

118

on until larger but still ordinary fish are taken. The really great spirits are never content until the depths of human experience have been plumbed and the wide expanses of human endeavor have been surveyed. Then, having decided which particular line of endeavor is most appealing—offers the best opportunity for pleasant labor and promise of largest returns, both for one's self and for society as a whole—they settle down to the business of preparing to use the 'tackle' needed in search of the 'big success' in the chosen field. They press on in the acquisition of skill never greatly discouraged if the desired ends are not immediately forthcoming, knowing all the while the thrilling pleasure which anticipation of the big catch, sure to come some day, always brings.

"Whoever starts the business of living, knowing that he who seeketh findeth (Matt. 7:7), and being inspired and impelled by that sacred truth, will some day know the thrilling experience of overcoming big obstacles and eventually of taking from the sea of human endeavor some worthy prize.

"The especial inference from the words of Jesus, 'and I will make you to become fishers of men' (Mark 1:17), is: 'When you have become my disciples you will put into your work of soul-winning the fine strategy of fishing. You will know that it is almost as foolish to go out calling unsaved people to come to your church houses and other places of worship as it would be to sit on the bank and call the fish to come and get worms or minnows from your dry hand. You will learn that a church building, whether simple tabernacle or ornate temple, is primarily a place for worship and for instruction and inspiration, wherein the man of God 'may be perfected, thoroughly furnished unto all good works'! (II Tim. 3:17, marginal reading). You will not, therefore, expect unregenerate people to come in any appreciable numbers to your church houses; hence you will always be diligent in seeking to obey your Lord's command, 'Go . . . make disciples.' 'Tis an inexpressible tragedy that so many millions of the followers of Christ never seem to learn that their business is to get out and seek the lost where they are, knowing that sooner or later from their number choice souls will be turned to Christ."

A Persistent Worker

Another vital lesson which fishing teaches is: There is big need for persistent efforts on the part of one who would succeed at any worth-while task or undertaking. What fisherman has not sat by the hour, trying various ways of catching fish and always to no avail? Yet what persistent fisherman has not known the thrill of being rewarded for patience by catching a goodly fish after such a long, fruitless effort? Every skilled angler of the past centuries would paraphrase the old and familiar adage thus: "If at first you catch no fish, cast, cast again!" Even as "faint heart ne'er won fair lady," so does the easily discouraged man or woman catch no big fish.

Out in a field one day a farmer and four sons were hoeing corn. They walked along together, digging out crabgrass and weeds where plows had not reached, chopping down stray sassafras and persimmon sprouts and thinning each hill of young corn to one stalk. It was monotonous work, but none of the four knew it. For them it was just routine labor, a part of the inescapable toil required in the production of food and feed. As they went to and fro across the field, they often worked for long periods without speaking a word. During such times muscles were tiring but brains were resting. At intervals some question asked or some casual remark made brought on an interesting discussion, sometimes a heated argument. When the conversation grew animated, hoe handles became props against which weary frames leaned, and muscles rested while brains worked.

On this particular day the group had nearly completed a field and there were yet two hours of sunshine, so there was no hurry. Following a long, quiet spell, the father paused, after having cleaned around a stump on his row, and asked, "What are you fellows going to do when you become men?"

Then followed a long and at times heated discussion about the relative merits of the various vocations mentioned. Many questions about what one would have to do in preparing for each vocation were fired at the parent who answered as fully as he could. Finally, he interrupted an argument about who made the more money, the banker or the doctor, and said: "The thing you boys must get straight is not so much the ease or the difficulty to be met in plying any trade or practicing any calling; not how much money it will pay you, but what will it cost you to make good? If you desire to be a good merchant, banker, lawyer, farmer, doctor, or minister, you must know that a long, hard road lies before you. You cannot attain such a worthy goal without hard work and long, persistent efforts. There is no royal road to success, the old adage says, and in your case it might well read, There is no riding-plow between you and a good harvest."

The years slipped rapidly by. One lad did become a banker. Another boy made preparation to be a merchant but was prevented by premature accidental death. The third saw the long, hard road to a medical degree and came to feel that he could never finance the trip, so stopped after two years in college. The fourth pressed on toward his goal. No task was too lowly for his hands if it provided a way for a few more hours in school, for another step toward the coveted diploma which would bring the privilege of pleading cases before the bar of public opinion. It cost him long hours of hard labor, often at the most menial tasks. It exacted of him weeks and months of self-denial, often demanding that he live for days on oatmeal porridge and toast made from stale bread. It robbed him of many contacts with fellow students, making him much of the time little more than a hermit, and often sending deep, biting nostalgia to tempt him to quit and go home to loved ones and to the ease and peace of the farm.

121

But he didn't quit! He wouldn't quit! By degrees the steep climb was made. When he grew discouraged and was on the verge of surrender, some sustaining hand would come and buoy his spirit, adding new hope and restoring the grim determination to press on. Fishing for him resulted on some days only in "dry hauls"; on other days there were nibbles and small strikes. Occasionally, when he had won a medal or some other honor came his way, he was thrilled by the big "catch," and wrote to his loved ones about it. All the while he was keeping in mind the "tarpon" about which he had so often dreamed, and which came, when at fifty years of age, he had climbed high in his profession and was honored by being made head of a great concern, and by having honorary degrees conferred upon him. After the years of preparation, he went out with a contract in one hand and the treasured diploma in the other, smiling at friends who surrounded him, while inwardly he was exulting because he had not stopped when days were so hard and the indications of success so meager.

The Fisher of Men

"It is imperative that fishers of men learn what persistence means," Time continued. "One of the most difficult things one ever may undertake is to persuade an unregenerate man that he needs a Saviour; and little less difficult, if any, is the task of persuading an unchurched Christian that he should align himself with the followers of Christ and cease to live with the worldly group. He who endeavors to be a soul-winner must be so sure of himself, so thoroughly convinced that his mission is a holy one which must not be ignored, and be so desperately in earnest, that he inevitably becomes an ardent salesman, who knows how to boost his product and will not be silenced for long in his talk for his Lord.

"For more than fifty years a certain mother prayed for the salvation of one of her sons. She would not let loose 'the horns of the altar' until her petition was granted, and when, at the age of eighty-four, she heard him make his confession of faith, her joy was almost more than her frail frame could endure. A woman of Wilson County, North Carolina, pleaded daily for her wayward husband from the time they were married until their children were adults and had homes of their own. Some smiled whenever, during a special prayer service, she asked others to join her in prayer for him. Then one evening, after thirty-five years had passed, that man surprised everybody at church when he strode down the aisle, made a frank confession of his sins, and dedicated his old, worn, sin-marred body to God.

" 'The effectual, fervent prayer of a righteous man availeth much' (James 5:16), and the persistent, earnest prayer of any saint, coupled with no less earnest and persistent work, will eventually result in God's fishers landing almost anyone who may be found along the stream of time.

"Mother Nature holds in her vast zoological gardens and aquaria hosts of interesting creatures, and from each of them man may learn valuable lessons. Only the vain egotist and the intellectual snob will ignore lessons which may be learned from her. The Master Teacher often drew from her ample lap some creature or thing through which to impart a lesson to His disciples. Thus the grains of wheat, the sparrow, the candle, the pearl, yeast, soil, stones—these and many others were immortalized by Him when He used each in turn in presenting to man a needed lesson. If, then, He found Nature providing so much for His teaching, man is unwise if he fails to gather from her such valuable lessons as those which may be learned from the fine art of angling, never forgetting that there can be no more thrilling and noble sport for the children of the King than that of fishing for men.

"For ages man has known the art of fishing and the ways of some at least of the finny tribe," old sage Time concluded. "Wherever he can find enough water to sustain his life, he will find something in the streams or pools for which to fish.

The wisdom of the great Teacher in choosing to liken the labors of discipleship to fishing is quite evident. And one might go on to show that, just as good fishers always catch fish, so do good disciples always secure trophies with which to honor their Master, hence they make sure that death will not rob them of all for which they have spent their time and efforts while here on earth."

CHAPTER NINE

The Anchor Holds

Asleep at Sea

Oops! I wonder if we're going to run head on into that little boat!"

It was the morning of July 4, 1913, and the steamer Pocahontas was heading out of Chesapeake Bay into Hampton Roads just as the sun was beginning to roll its fiery disk out of the sea and when the heavens were bedecked with a color ensemble such as I had never before seen. Suddenly the pilot had changed course, veering directly toward an anchored craft.

I had been awake most of the night, for it was my first steamer journey, my first time to see the ocean, my first time to see a sunrise at sea. Down under the bridge, with the pilot's steady hand and trained eye above me, I had stood watching the swell of the bay, the lights along the shore, and the slowly fading stars. When the rays of the sun began to break over the rim of the sea and to spread fan-like athwart the gray skies, my soul experienced a new and indescribable pleasure.

While I was watching the morning light change with fascinating rapidity and listening to the swishing of the waters as they were cut by the prow of the Pocahontas, I noticed several

125

WHERE DOES THE ANCHOR GO?

smaller craft at anchor. We passed close enough to one of these for me to see sailors asleep on the deck. Momentarily I was lost in daydreams while childhood desires to know the sea and ships returned and demanded attention. It was during my musing that I happened to look up to see the prow of our ship turn directly toward the smaller boat. To a landlubber it was an exciting moment before the pilot again moved the tiller and the seeming danger was past.

When the course was changed and I was assured of safety, I went over to the starboard rail and followed it aft, watching the small boat slip by. Soon it was rocking in our wake, and I wondered if the sailors would be aroused and if they would be frightened. I could see them quite plainly, and none seemed even to move. Years later I spent several days at sea and then learned more about seamen than I had known before. After having had that experience, I could look back with keener appreciation to the voyage on the Pocahontas and pictures of the smaller craft in Hampton Roads.

After the passing of a good many years, memories of the quiet, early morning waters in the noted Virginia port have lost some insignificant details; but basic facts now stand out all the more clearly, presenting valuable lessons. Impressions made upon my youthful spirit that Independence Day morning have remained to add both pleasure and profit to living by helping to clarify certain fundamental truths upon which the happiest and most profitable living is dependent. Father Time thus once more comes with a helpful voice.

Secure Moorings

"Consider the boats anchored here and there about the lower bay and out in Hampton Roads. They tell of peace and rest which trustworthy anchorage alone can give the human spirit. The seamen sleeping on the somewhat frail ships had no restless hours because of fear. The slight swell produced by a passing steamer served only to lull them into deeper slumber. They lived and moved and had their being with the sea, hence, had adapted themselves to its moods. A severe storm might bring to some of them grave concern about their safety, but the ordinary squall and the swell stirred up by it was no more to them than an April shower to a landsman. They were assured of safety because they trusted their moorings. The anchor upon which any crew depends furnishes a striking parallel to 'the anchor of the soul that is both sure and steadfast' (Heb. 6:9). Learn of it!

"First, much depends upon where the anchor goes when dropped. The seamen do not see the bottom to which they send the anchor when they wish to have security for a season without going to a pier. They cannot know what is down there, twenty, forty, ninety fathoms beneath the surface. They do not need to know; all that interests them is the fact that other anchors have found secure hold in those depths. They may sometimes ask themselves what is down in the depths; occasionally, one of them is curious enough to look the matter up in a report of the government *Coast and Geodetic Survey*. But the majority of the sailors never bother their heads about such things. The anchor strikes and holds fast! That is enough!

"Night after night men on harbor craft sleep peacefully inside Hampton Roads and hundreds of other ports. Seldom does a storm strike there, and usually if one comes, it gives advance notice of its approach. The tide comes and goes, but it is seldom high enough to cause any concern inside the sheltered retreat. A storm may strike suddenly during the night, as sometimes happens in any port, but seamen can go to their cabins below and sleep on. The invisible bed of the sea is a secure place to which to be fastened, and passing ages have proved the reliability of anchor and chain. A well-equipped ship is too safe to leave one a victim of worry.

"How readily does the illustration apply to the spiritual nature of mankind and its need for safety! On that memorable morning you wished to ask the seamen, 'Aren't you afraid to spend your nights out here with only the small anchor and its smaller cable to protect you from drifting into the open sea or into the path of some passing ship? Aren't you afraid the cable may break or the anchor slip?' Had you asked such questions, the men would have smiled at the landlubber and answered with an emphatic 'No, we are not afraid; we have tested that anchor and know that it will hold. But even if it should not do so, we have another safeguard, a watchman who stands awake while we are asleep.'

"A wise captain never forgets that there is a possibility that a defect in the anchor chain may develop or that some unusual weather conditions may develop with high wind or an unusually strong tide. Possible emergencies are provided for by the watch which each ship sets, especially when in a traffic zone. An anchor alone will bring a sense of security to seamen, but perfect confidence that all will be well under any circumstances is had when the anchor is supplemented by the observant eye of a good guard.

"One of the calls familiar to all who love stories of the days of sailships was that of the watchman who, when he had sounded time by striking the ship's bell, would chant in this manner, 'Four bells and all is well aboard the ————,' naming the ship. Should a serious storm appear to be going to strike them, or should any other grave danger be impending, the watchman was honor-bound to sound the alarm, so that all could make ready. The seamen trusted him because they knew him and understood full well that he, whoever he might be at the time, was vitally interested in their welfare, that his honor and probably his life were at stake and could be forfeited by carelessness or by neglect of duty. They trusted him and thus were doubly assured of safety.

The Soul's Anchorage

"Now look at your own experience in the light of the seamen and their dependence upon the anchor and the watchman. It is not reasonable for man to suppose that there is no means whereby he may secure his frail spiritual craft while navigating life's 'wild, restless sea.' Many an adult learned while a child in Sunday school that God has provided everyone a solid basis for hope. It is a significant day for one when he turns by the exercise of faith and puts his dependence for spiritual security in Jesus Christ, the Rock of Ages. A child readily takes the step, if properly instructed. Instinctively, the boy and girl know that God is; it is easy to show them that sin exists and that it destroys the ties between the rational creature and the Creator upon which security depends. Fear of judgment for sin and natural desire for spiritual security lead the erring youth to repentance and to yield to the inner voice of faith.

"No philosophical speculations enter into the making of this decision. Such mental hurdles as the philosopher must pass come with maturing years and the expanding contacts which they bring. A lad knows by instinct that God is; it is not difficult to convince the child that he is a sinner, estranged from God and in danger of judgment. Quite naturally, therefore, he is easily led to 'lay hold on the hope set before us' (Heb. 6:8), turning to Christ for the peace and security which He alone can give.

"There can be no absolute trust in the security of this anchorage, however, until the believer becomes aware of the fact that the Redeemer is ever mindful of His own; hence, that the Holy Spirit is sent to be the Watchman who makes sure that, if the anchorage should slip or faith release its hold for a while upon the Rock of Ages, the craft will not be allowed to founder or drift far away. It is a bright day for anyone when he puts his immortal self under the covenant of grace by faith in the Lord Jesus Christ. It is a brighter day when one who has done this discovers how much dependence he may put in that anchor because its protection is made perfect by the watchful eye of the Holy Spirit who not only watches over God's own when they are resting at anchor, but has oversight of the steering when any voyage is being made.

"Knowing that He is ever present, it should readily become the fixed desire of every believer to have Him warn against the breakers, rip tides, and other perils which sin brings along the way and to show the safe courses of conduct to be developed into fixed habits of life. He knows the way every believer should travel; He understands how weak and impotent is the will of everyone who undertakes to follow in His train; He, therefore, would insure the hope and assure the peace of all by letting them know that He is on guard, that when the Redeemer promised, 'I will never leave thee nor forsake thee,' He meant just exactly what He said (Heb. 13:5).

Certain Hope

"Look for a little while at the believer's hope; see it as it enters into that within the veil; learn to feel its sway over human fears and doubts; be assured of the never-failing source of security which God has provided; discover these things and you may know the peace that passeth all understanding, the inspiration that will lift with unfailing arm above the obstacles and bring victory over the enemies which every follower of Christ must incur along his way, the last one being death. Remember!

"First of all, the soul's anchor reaches the unseen. Do what he will, go where he may, man can never remove from the human family the certainty that God is, or destroy the assurance that inexorable justice is as inseparable a trait of His nature as is love. It is impossible to produce children who do not enter life with an inner conviction that there is a supernatural Author of life and Creator of what Mother Nature holds in her ample lap. For generations there were places in the sea which man had never sounded, depths to which his sounding equipment had never reached. But all the while seamen knew that there was a bottom. One may imagine a bottomless hole, but he knows that there is no such thing.

"Likewise one knows that there has to be a 'bottom' or basis for everything. He may spend his entire life speculating about what the First Cause is, but he cannot thereby remove the cause or put an end to man's search for it. One man may be philosopher enough to go on in search of data upon which to base theories about the unknown beyond, and another may be theologian enough to seek to interpret the hypotheses which he and the philosopher set forth in explanation of the origin of what is seen; but the great mass of human beings, like the vast majority of seamen, are not concerned about such mental calisthenics. They know that God is, that there is something within themselves which is immortal, and that they need somehow to find a way to connect it with the unknown wherein the Spirit of the living God is dominant.

"Science, philosophy, theology—all fail to reveal to the mind the secrets which lie beyond the veil. The wise man will not, therefore, spend much precious time trying to uncover the mysteries of the spiritual deep. You should have learned long ago that you cannot enter it while in the flesh; you cannot fathom its depths with any mental sounding device at your command; you cannot peer through the mazes that separate it from your inner eyes; the dividing line was set by the Creator, and the only way by which you can reach what is beyond it is by the exercise of faith."

Again I knew that I was learning basic truth. I cannot see it, but I know that a dependable source of security is there beyond the reach of the natural senses. When my anchor gripped that Rock, my faith embedded itself in Him, then I felt the peace which security alone gives. Tides of religious fanaticism have come and gone out; currents of strange ideas have beat about my spiritual craft; all kinds of heretical influences have tugged at my heart, seeking to pull me from my anchorage; foolish religionists have passed by with their mental creations troubling the waters where I was anchored; winds of temptation have often blown, sometimes causing me to fear that all was not well; indeed, hours have come along when Satan sneered at me through the darkness, seeming to take fiendish delight in my distress and consternation of soul. But whenever I have begun to drift out to the open sea, the anchor has held! My craft is brought up short, and I am stirred to the depths of my soul by the sense of security which the promises of God bring to me.

I felt the anchor hold one day in 1912 when an offer of a very attractive job was made by the company for which I had been working that summer, an opening which would have ended my preparation for the ministry. It brought anew, and more strongly than ever before, the temptation to get away from God and His insistent demand for me to prepare for a life of sacrificial service. Just when I was ready to accept the proffered position, there came a telegram from the pastor of the First Baptist Church of Durham, North Carolina, Dr. John Peter Hurt, telling me that he had secured for me a fellowship in Trinity College (now Duke University) and bidding me report for duty September 11! Often have I wondered, "If that friend had not been used of God during that critical period of my life, what would have happened to me?"

Looking back across the years since youth, scores of incidents are brought from memory, each bearing unquestionable testimony to the certainty that God does provide "ministering angels" (Ps. 34:7; 91:11; Heb. 1:14) who care for His children, sometimes interfering suddenly with their plans, sometimes administering chastisement, often blocking a path along which wayward feet would fain travel. One should know God's willingness to shield from harm and thus be more earnest and persistent in his petition, "And lead us not into temptation." If the anchor does not hold against the winds of ambition as well as against the tides of carnal desires, then it has not gripped the Rock of Ages.

"Somewhere in the great sweeping reaches of the unknown," says Father Time, "God has set the Rock, and faith may take

133

hold of it. Man does not need to see Him face to face; he does not have to look beyond the veil which separates the natural from the spiritual; it should be enough for him to know that after the anchor has held for so long, after it has made secure the craft of so many others, it will hold his life. No more should the mysteries connected with the person and work of the Redeemer cause the believer to distrust his faith than do the unknown facts about the seabed cause the trained seamen to distrust their anchor."

I learned a third precious truth from the study of the parallel between the seaman's hope and that of my soul, and that is to know the added security which is provided by the continuous eye of a faithful Watchman in Zion. "Aren't you afraid you will not hold out?" I am sometimes asked. "Aren't you afraid your trust may prove to be deceptive and thus your hope prove vain?" To such questions I have at last learned to reply, much as the sailors would have replied to my foolish questions about their sense of security, "No! I am not afraid, for I have not only a safe anchorage but a Watchman who has promised never to leave me nor forsake me" (Gen. 28:15; Heb. 13:5).

Surely man can trust One who has been attending his way throughout so many centuries. He who was with the Father in the process of creation (Prov. 8:22, 31; John 1:1; Rev. 19:13 R.V.) has promised to guide His own with His eye (Ps. 32:8; 33:18). He guarantees security to all whom the Father has given Him (Ps. 37:28; John 10:29; Phil. 1:6). Assurance of the protection of the Almighty is given in Paul's declaration, "Your life is hid with Christ in God" (Col. 3:3), and "sealed with the Holy Spirit of promise until the day of redemption" (Eph. 1:13, 14). The anchor is sure and holds the believer at all times (I Peter 1:5)!

"The watch was set in eternity," my ancient teacher concludes, "and so careful is He that not even a sparrow falleth without being observed (Matt. 10:29). Surely, in response to the Master's 'How much more are ye better than the fowls?' (Matt.

6:24) any human being should be able to respond, 'Vastly more, dear Lord. Help me, therefore, both to rely upon Thy care and to be diligent and tireless in seeking to develop that which has been restored in me through the New Birth. Upon Thee who hath restored my soul, I shall rely with unquestioning faith, fearing no more to leave the going in Thy hands, thereby making it possible to give a more productive and a happier service to Thee!' "

How good it is to have such a hope, one that enters into that within the veil (Heb. 6:19)! Our God has sought, by basing His promises upon two immutable things, to assure all His spiritual children of their security in Him (Heb. 6:16–18). Whoever, therefore, turns his faith toward the realm of the spirit and there fastens it about the Rock of Ages has a hope that is not fragile, a haven free from peril, an anchorage that is adamant! God has given assurance of that fact! Jesus Christ the Redeemer has emphasized it! So let us turn with Isaac Watts, the writer of a great old hymn, and sing with untrammeled spirits,

> Unshaken as the sacred hills,
> And fixed as mountains be;
> Firm as a rock the soul shall rest
> That leans, O Lord, on Thee.
>
> Nor walls nor hills could guard so well
> Old Salem's happy ground,
> As those eternal arms of love
> That every saint surround.
>
> Firm as the earth Thy Gospel stands,
> My Lord, my hope, my trust;
> If I am found in Jesus' hands
> My soul can ne'er be lost!

For all who have trusted their souls to Jesus the Redeemer and who have made Him Lord of their lives, this sentiment can be appropriated, and thus the grim shadows of death may be dissipated.

How Could a Worm Do That?

CHAPTER TEN

From Cocoons to God

A Lad's Curiosity

Look at these peculiar cocoons, Dad. There are several of them under the bark of this post. Are they like those from which our silk comes?"

These questions were asked one day by a husky sixteen-year-old lad in a southern home. He and his father were clearing bushes and briers from the fence which enclosed one of their fields. While resting for a few minutes the boy had pulled from a post some loose bark, thus exposing the silken bags which caterpillars had spun about themselves weeks before.

"Those are cocoons of a native moth," his father replied, "and not of the silkworm, which does not live here. However, the little bags are made of silk."

"Why don't we cultivate the moth and develop our own silk industry?" the lad asked, pulling at some strands which he had loosened from one of the cocoons.

"That's a problem for you to figure out later," replied his father. "It is probable that the silk itself is of an inferior grade. It may be that the caterpillars could not be raised in large enough numbers to make a paying venture of their culture. So far, we in America have found too many other profitable enterprises to feel any need for extended experiments with silk."

"Tell me about it, Dad," the boy urged after a moment's silence. "Just what is a cocoon and how is it formed?"

His father asked for one of the silken bags, laid it upon the palm of his left hand and rolled it back and forth a few times under his right forefinger. He was not a trained naturalist, but he had been a diligent student of nature and had learned enough to know many of the phenomena which arouse inquisitive minds everywhere. After a few moments of musing he said:

"In this lies one of the great secrets of the natural world, my boy. No one knows the 'Why?' of it; man can only observe and speculate about the 'How?' Last spring what you called a butterfly was flitting in the sun somewhere near here and sucking nectar from the flowers, as you have so often seen them do. Really, it was a moth, and it spent a great deal of time laying eggs on plant leaves. These eggs readily turned into larvae or tiny worms or caterpillars.

"When each had eaten its fill, a strange thing happened to it. It somehow responded to an inner urge to stop eating and to hunt for a place where it would be sheltered during the days ahead."

"But how could a worm know to do that?" the boy interrupted. "I can see how it would know when its 'tummy' was filled, but not what would be a safe place or when it was time to hunt one. Furthermore, how would it know where to go to find such a spot?"

"It would be a wonderful experience, Son, if man could discover a way by which he could learn just what does take place in the nerve centers of a caterpillar to let it know when to stop eating, and what sensations within drive it to a place of shelter before it begins to spin its cocoon. Some caterpillars bore into the ground before spinning. One species from which certain 'shepherd ants' secure 'milk'—a sweet liquid which exudes from

138

the worm's body during its feeding stage—are protected by the herdsmen while descending from the feeding place on tree boughs. A regular 'guard detail' attends each caterpillar until it has opened its tunnel and disappeared in it. They then close and seal the hole and carefully camouflage the spot before leaving. They seem somehow to know that next year's food supply is dependent upon the worm that has served them so well. This species of ant, like its agricultural cousin, has a brain larger in proportion to its body than that of any other animate creature."

"Is it possible that such ants can think and plan, can work out problems as man does?"

"We do not know," his father replied. "It seems far more reasonable to think that they act in obedience to fixed laws of nature and not as a result of reason and advance planning. But whatever the fact, we can know that such creatures as caterpillars, wasps, termites, and others all about us do follow courses already set for them, methods of labor which are intelligible. It may be that the caterpillars have unusually keen vision, hence can detect from a distance just the proper place to which to go before spinning the cocoons.

The Big Mystery

"The big mystery connected with the caterpillar is not found in the few evidences of intelligence which it presents to man; it is seen in what takes place after the inner warning lets it know that feasting hours are ended. Keep in mind that last summer a wrinkled, hairy worm crawled up and attached itself to this post. Then it did something which no human being could ever do—built this cocoon out of material which its digestive organs created, and somehow wound this silken bag about itself, making, it is said, more than 250,000 turns of its body in weaving the outer shell first and the downy inner layers last.

"What happened to that worm when its cocoon was completed is a mystery which, so far as man goes, is a real miracle. For hundreds of years scientists have been trying to figure it out. Let's cut this cocoon in two—there! What do you see?"

"Just some gooey liquid," the boy replied, after peering closely at what lay on his father's palm. "Do you mean that the caterpillar went to pieces, or dissolved into that stuff?"

"Exactly!" replied the man. "I am told that a powerful microscope will show the stuff inside a live cocoon to be a mass of living cells, each and all held together for weeks only by the cocoon. Just how or why the caterpillar goes to pieces as it does no one can say, except people who believe in God, the Creator, and who know that He has made everything on our planet, each after its kind, and hence is subject to definite laws which govern its nature, its physical form, its method of reproduction, and the kind of service it does in the vast field of living things; in other words, what its life cycle shall be."

"But what became of the caterpillars legs, jaws, hairs and all? There's no sign of them in this shell," the boy asked after he had picked up half the cocoon and examined its inside very carefully.

"What becomes of the yolk and white of an egg which a hen or the incubator hatches?" his father replied. "It is transformed by a tiny life cell into a baby fowl. How? Ask that question for a thousand years and there will be but one answer: 'It does it because of the operation of natural law.' Even so, the whole caterpillar, acting in obedience to a law of life, goes to pieces —disintegrates is a big word for it—and for many weeks the cells which once made up the worm remain in a state of suspended animation, that is, the life in them remains at rest. Hot, dry sun, or cold, continuous rains, ice, zero weather—none of these seems to affect the cells of this particular moth.

"But wait until the warm spring days like this come along; then the cells begin to wake up. Take some of those cocoons to the barn and put them in a secure place where you can watch them. When all danger of frost and of cold, raw days has passed, the cells in each will reassemble, and soon a new creature will cut through one end of the cocoon—a moth exactly like that which last spring laid the egg from which this creature grew."

"How can that be, Dad?" the boy exclaimed. "How can this gooey stuff change itself into a beautifully colored flying thing? How do the cells know when to make the moth? Do the cells that once formed the caterpillar's head, make the moth's head, those from the legs make moth legs? What cells make the dainty wings, and which the long snout with which the moth sucks the nectar from flowers? What makes the cells turn out a moth instead of a butterfly or a wasp? When—"

"Wait a minute, Son!" his dad exclaimed. "You have begun a chain of questions which has no end, for each presupposes or demands an answer which involves another question like it. Only when one gets back to the beginning and there finds a creative Spirit great enough to account for the plan by which the creatures are made and for the rules or laws under which the plan is carried out—only then can he find an answer to the 'What?' and the 'Why?' that stare at one every time he meets a mystery such as life, or beauty, or harmony, or anything else which you can find about you.

The Growing Glory

"The scientific name for what takes place in the world when a worm becomes a moth or butterfly, or a maggot grows into a beetle, is 'Metamorphosis' (*meta,* over or again, and *morphe,* to form or make) that is, a changing from one form to another. How it occurs who can explain? Why the Creator decreed that certain creatures should pass through such a cycle no one knows. It pleased God to see that His infinite nature, His omniscient mind, and His omnipresent hand should be utilized in the production of an innumerable host of things and an incomprehensible display of variety among inanimate as well as the living things of the earth."

"I wonder why He did it that way?" the boy quietly asked more of himself than of his father, who had resumed work. No

141

purely natural basis or explanation could be found for the phenomenon, but interest in it already aroused in the lad's mind did not wane. When he quit work that evening he took with him a piece of bark to which some cocoons hung. He stored it in a safe place and watched until patience was rewarded by seeing one moth come forth, stretch, and dry her wings and fly away. While in college he made a special study of insects and once more the question, "Why should a moth come from a caterpillar by way of a cocoon?" came to challenge his mind. Four decades have passed since then. Interesting years have given a chance to secure from Father Time some helpful lessons and sublime truths.

"The longer one studies the strange cycle of life anywhere," Father Time assures us, "the more convinced he must become that the Creator made it mysterious and gave it variety in order that He might reveal to man some fundamental facts about his Maker and also to provide so many inexplicable mysteries in the natural realm that only foolish people would seek to ignore or deny the miraculous involved in the realm of the spirit. You may be sure also that God intended to open windows through which man's soul may catch glimpses of itself and its future and have assurance that one's belief in immortality is not a foolish whim. If you keep your mind free from enslaving complexes, refuse to be cowed or daunted by the sneers and taunting questions of infidels, agnostics, and other people whose souls have been locked behind walls of materialism, you will be able all along to hear truth as she proclaims through Nature as well as through the pages of Holy Scripture messages of vital moment which will strengthen your heart, exalt your spirit and give direction and continuous zest to the business of living.

A Message of Change

"You cannot watch the various expressions which life presents about you without being struck by the certainty of planned change. What appears today will be different tomorrow. What tomorrow may present to you will be but a prophecy of that which will come later on. The moth flitted in the sunshine for a few days. It played in the gardens and fields for a little while. It deposited its quota of eggs and, having served Nature's purpose, dropped off some plant and died. Then came the worm. It feasted for a few hours until it had reached a certain stage in its development, when it turned from feasting to hunt a place for its cocoon. Its service as a larva had been completed when the cocoon was finished.

"Change continued after the spinning ceased. Gradually the cells separated themselves and became dormant. One seems to see inside the cocoon only a small mass of protoplasm. The average person never knows that it is a host of living cells waiting for the hand of the Creator to arouse the cells and bid them assemble in new form. Surely, there is something in this strange cycle—these changes—which demands that rational beings admit the existence of more than the working of purely physical factors! How can one see this change, always so accurately repeated, and not know that its steps were planned in advance and guided all along, age after age, by a creative mind which has to be outside of and far above the creature which changes?

"Hear another word," Father Time seems to demand of us. "The cocoon with its strange metamorphosis involves a predetermined course of activity. By no process can man change the nature of this particular moth so that its larvae will develop into moths without the grub or caterpillar stage. The grub, the silk, the cocoon, the period of suspended animation, the reassembly of cells—the whole cycle is inherent in the life-spark which is planted in the moth's eggs. Here is one of countless proofs of predestination, and man should not be foolish enough to ignore it. For if the Author of life determined in advance the times and seasons, and made sure what is to emerge from every fertilized ovum when it is permitted to develop, how much more certainly has He determined what shall be the ultimate end of creation as a whole?

143

"All too little attention has been paid to Paul's declaration, 'The whole creation groaneth and travaileth in pain together until now—and even we ourselves [redeemed souls] groan within ourselves, waiting for the adoption, to wit, the redemption of our body (Rom. 8:22, 23). The apostle saw the unrest in Nature as the counterpart of the unrest in man's soul, both of them testifying that out ahead is a new world with new laws governing it. Everywhere Nature is calling attention to the certain fact that everything, whether small or great, is pressing on toward some prearranged goal. Foolish indeed are men who close their minds to this fact, hence refuse to believe that beyond the flesh lies a larger and more wonderful existence for all rational beings who have sense enough to prepare for it.

"If there is any value whatever in 'preponderance of evidence,' surely no sensible person would leave the jury box without having had his opinion about the future of life determined to a large extent by the fact that everywhere in all ages rational beings have felt that existence in the flesh is not the whole of man's experience. Something in the caterpillar made it react in definite ways because its mission had not ended when it had gorged itself upon foliage. It would be foolish to surmise that it could rationalize, hence, by a process of reasoning reach the important decision which led to the cocoon. It acted as a result of instinct or implanted nature. But the conclusion reached through this instinct was absolutely logical, and it resulted each time in a new set of acts which culminated in the production of a moth. It is, therefore, entirely sensible for one to declare, 'Instinctive or implanted knowledge is, on the whole, more reliable than man's fickle, and so often abortive, processes of ratiocination.' The hunter who becomes lost must follow his dog or horse if he ever gets out of the woods on a starless night, because instinct in its sphere is far more reliable than reason.

"What, then, will wise people say about the world-wide, age-old certainty in human hearts that death of the body does not end all for the spirit of man? No people has yet been found who did not know by instinct two vital things, namely: God is, and man's spirit or soul is immortal. The fact that religions are often very base and animistic does not disprove this. Is it any more reasonable for one to accept as a scientific fact the certainty of the inner urge or instinct which drives a worm to spin a cocoon or leads a lower animal unerringly to its home, than it is to accept as valid the inner urge of the human family for God? Is it any more reasonable to accept the fact that the life of the moth predestines the acts involved in metamorphosis than it is to reason that the life in man predestines a resurrection of his body?

"Will there be any greater mystery in the transformation of his dust into a spiritual body than there is in the transformation of chemical elements into his physical body? Is any more of a miracle involved in the continuance of his life or spirit between the death and the resurrection of his body than there is in the continuance of the life of the moth during the cocoon stage, or in the continuance from three to seventeen years of the life of certain beetles in their dormant larvae, or in the life of a grain of Egyptian wheat, dormant for two and a half millennia?

"Certainly there is not! Foolish indeed is the human being who allows his youthful instinctive knowledge of God to atrophy and die because of lack of cultivation. Irrational indeed is the idea that, because one can think himself into a state of skepticism and even of rank infidelity, he has thereby altered the cycle for all mankind, abolished immortality and destroyed God. Just as the age-long continuance of the mysterious cycle of metamorphosis bears inescapable and undeniable testimony to the fact of the guiding hand of an abiding creative Spirit, even so does man's cycle of life, with its recurrent initial outreach for its Maker, bear inescapable and undeniable testimony to the fact that life in the flesh is for man only the initial and preparatory stage in his whole existence. Made for the praise and glory of his Creator, man finds no satisfaction for his restless soul until he finds it in fellowship with his Creator and in contemplation of

145

the thrilling certainty that the final stage in his changes will be the resurrection of his body and the restoration both of the ideal nature which Eden saw when creation began and of the fellowship with God for which the creature was made and especially endowed.

The Great Climax

"Hear one other bit of wisdom, found in the lessons which Natural History is always ready to teach," says Father Time. "Stated in simple words it is: 'From the voiceless cells within the cocoon, or any other place of life, comes the assurance of the ages that the immortality of man's spirit is no fiction of primitive minds passed on generation after generation by inescapable laws of evolution.'

"If one would comprehend more accurately the nature of life itself, let him compare his cycle with that of the moth. If we imagine that the moth which produced these cocoons is the offspring of moths that were here 20,000 years ago, we would have to figure man's existence at some 600,000 years, since a moth's generation is one year and man's about thirty. Or compare it with the cycle of some microscopic germ whose generation is only four hours—six generations for every day—and one would run into a length of years almost passing comprehension. The thing of great moment, therefore, is not what form life takes in manifesting itself; not how long or short is the cycle of life anywhere; but what is the life and for what purpose does it exist? *Either life is eternal or else it was created;* that is axiomatic. If it was made, then it has an Author, and all reason assures one that it has a definite purpose in and behind it. That purpose must help us understand it.

"Quite evidently moths serve mankind in two major ways: first, helping perpetuate certain useful plants by aiding them in the reproductive process; and secondly, by providing silk fibers. The fact that only a few species produce silk in usable quantities no more argues against design in their creation than does the

146

fact that only a fraction of the sun's heat reaches our planet argues against design in its form and place in our universe. When, therefore, the end in view has been met, we can well believe that the moth-life will be discontinued. In other words, when no more flowers are to be pollenized and no more silk is needed by man, the moth will become extinct. Likewise will it be with all other lower creatures; having served their day, they will cease to be.

"Bear in mind always that there is but one sensible opinion about the life of man with all its wonderful attributes, and that is, it is made for eternal purposes or ends. In the Book of Genesis we are told that man was created not to perform a mere temporary function, but to fill a larger mission by being a co-operative worker with his Creator, having dominion over all the world. Only during the twentieth century since Christ, however, has he begun to discover just how vast are those resources, how infinite their variety and uses, and how incomprehensible the power latent in Nature's garb.

"Along with the discovery and utilization of the natural resources has gone the discovery of vast spiritual resources. The outreach of man's mind, the extent to which the reasoning faculties may be developed, the increasing certainty that mind is capable of transmitting its product—sense impressions—long distances by what is called mental telepathy; clairvoyance, occultism, and acceptance by cultured folks of the theories of spiritism—these and other phenomena of our day join their voices with those of theists of every age in support of the inescapable belief in a spiritual realm for which man is peculiarly endowed, hence, was quite evidently formed or predestined.

Vital Implications

"Today the door is opening wide!" One can hear Father Time almost shout. "The discovery and utilization of atomic energy have exploded many infidel theories and made inescapable a belief in the infinite power of an omnipotent Spirit. The flash of a radar signal to the moon and the returning echo made inescapable one's belief in the infinite sway of mind over matter, hence, in an omniscient Spirit. The universe, expanding before the ever-enlarging mechanical eye of man, bears witness to the reality of an omnipresent Spirit whose almighty hand alone can account for the vast and harmonious interplay of incalculable powers about you. The growing certainty in the minds, not only of prophets but of infidels, that our planet is hastening toward some catastrophic end should not and will not be ignored by sane thinkers when considering the problems of life and seeking to determine the course of future events.

"Shall rational beings see all these mysteries unfolding about them and keep their minds closed to the spiritual implications involved? When by the fission of the atom the inconceivable stores of power in the universe have been released, would anyone higher in mental scale than a moron believe that the vast stores of energy are intended to remain forever with only finite minds to control and utilize them? With the increasing certainty among serious people that the world which we now know, including humanity, cannot abide forever, what could be more sensible or more logical than to accept as authoritative the revelation in the Bible which clearly sets out the origin, the purposes and the ultimate ends of the whole program of life?

"Somewhere, sometime, the 'spirits of just men made perfect' will step to the fore in keeping with the plan of the ages. Then that which today is mortal will have put on immortality, that which today is shackled by its temporal and physical dwelling place will have come into possession of a body which is immortal. Then will the mystery called death be swallowed up in victory!

"If it could rationalize, the grub would no doubt think of the day of release from its cocoon. The moth would find delight in reminiscences of the long, trying days inside its cocoon, having discovered that they were essential to the fuller, richer life. Even so, all who choose to suffer afflictions with the people of God (Heb. 11:25) anticipate their redemption and will some day

148

revel in memories of the privations and hardships experienced while in the tabernacle of clay, knowing that they were but stepping stones to the richer, fuller experiences intended for liberated souls.

"Unhappy must they be who refuse to believe that human life is very much like life in the cocoon in that it is a preparatory stage for the future! Foolish indeed are they who become so concerned about gratifying their carnal lusts that they lose sight of the ultimate end of life! Dangerously conceited are they who refuse to acknowledge the fact of, and the imperative need for, the Omnipotent, Omniscient, Omnipresent Creator and Lord of life, hence fail to respond to His directive will! They are gorging themselves upon temporal things and never thinking of or desiring the life for which the temporal should make way. Blinded by lusts of the flesh, beguiled by false teachers who make them disregard the basic needs of their souls, lured by the glamor of the passing show, they refuse to look ahead and to know that what they call Time is but a checkmark across the dial of eternity, and what they call pleasure is but a momentary tickling of their carnal ribs! Although made for fellowship with God, they develop only the carnal. In the end, instead of being called at death to a higher and more wonderful life and service, they are fit only to be cast entirely away from God, hence, are turned into Hell along with all who forget God (Ps. 9:17; Rev. 21:8).

"Never refuse to see the vital lessons which God has set before all who are made in His image. The mystery of life does not lie in the sprouting grain, the bursting nut, the metamorphosis of a moth, but in the Power which animates each implanted cell and starts it to multiplying under direction of a plan that makes certain results inevitable. Never be afraid of any ridicule which you may encounter when you express your faith in the Word of God, the only Book in all the libraries of man that sets forth a dogmatic yet logical explanation not only of the temporal world, but also of the beings for whom the world was made and to

149

whom the Eternal made it intelligible. He has made you and all other rational beings to have a place and a part in the unfolding drama of the ages.

"The ancient preacher was not dreaming when he wrote the beautiful tribute to old age, found in Ecclesiastes 12:2–7. He had caught a vision of eternal truth and set it forth for all subsequent ages to read and enjoy. The climax of that revelation is found in the words, 'Then shall the dust return to the earth as it was; and the spirit shall return unto God who gave it.' He was setting down some simple fundamentals, chief of which is: 'Man's experience which we call death is intended to be only a fitting climax to his life in the flesh. It is not a cessation of being nor an end to rationalizing; it is merely release from the cocoon inside which each immortal human spirit is predestined to spend a brief part of eternity.'

"When one can grasp the significance of that truth and act upon the basis which it sets up, he will make sure that his relation with God is right. Then he can abide in the shadow of the Almighty, knowing well that whatever may befall him while in the flesh will not remove the day when the chrysalis will be shed and he will go forth with freedom for more wonderful experiences, into a realm and relationship for which he was created and which is lost only when willful disregard of divine law and proffered redemption bring to the judgment one who has chosen to go some other way than the way of the cross."

It now seems ages since these happy days of childhood when one or the other parent sought to help satisfy the curiosity of growing children. When the cocoon was first examined imagination was rampant. It readily supplied the "missing link" between its mysteries and the Hand that produced them. Years of study produced questions and provided some answers that turned the mind from the Eternal in search of some more tangible *raison d'être* of metamorphosis. But now that the spirit is drawing near the day when it will experience the transformation decreed for it by the Creator, it begins to have "strange restless moments" when it feels that that which holds it to its lowly earth-bound prison is about to break and let it go free. After hearing Father Time's preachments, there is exuberance of heart and elation of mind that lead one to sing of the blessings which are in store for them who have followed the true Way.

SOME GLAD DAY

Some day the silver cord will break,
The pitcher crash on fountain's rim;
The cistern's wheel will no more creak,
And watchful eyes will have grown dim.
But joy 'twill bring to them who make
Their peace with God, His way shall take.

Some happy day the Christian's dream
Will be fulfilled. His house of clay
He'll leave, and that which now doth seem
Uncertain, vague and far away
Will greet his eager waiting eyes—
The glorious fields of Paradise!

Today the chrysalis. But wait!
Fear not the coming of the dark!
When death has opened wide the gate,
The soul in triumph may embark
Upon its flight from earth's hard hand
To God's eternal Canaan land!

WILD WATERS REVEAL TRUTH

CHAPTER ELEVEN

The Key to Heaven

Restless Waters

ONE AUGUST AFTERNOON in 1915 I drove from La Mesa to the famous playground of La Jolla, California. After looking over the place and watching the crowds that milled in and out of its curio shops and cafes, I went down to see the caves from which the town received its Spanish name. It is a wonderful spot where Nature has done her best through the centuries to make everything unusual and attractive.

I walked here and there, looking into crevices in the sandstone bluff which stands like a stern guard between the land and the restless Pacific. I crawled down into a break in the rocks and, bracing myself between two walls of stone, watched the waters as each incoming swell forced them through grottoes and tunnels where they crawled like great green serpents, hissing with each change in their ceaseless passing. The continuous roar of the breakers echoed from the caverns with a dull monotonous murmur, broken only by the distant laughter of carefree tourists who were sporting in the surf in the cove.

I left the caves, mounted the cliff, dug my initials into the stone among hundreds of other such, and then turned to watch the breakers. About a hundred yards out from the bluff where

I stood lay a pile of rock, broken off years before by the impact of some tidal wave. Over it the breakers jumped and sported as if jubilant over their fallen victim. Regularly the waters came in with a long, curling swell which rose with angry might as it neared the shore. When a breaker hit the stone rampart, there was a dull boom as if a cannon had been fired in Pluto's realm; the waters leaped into the air, scattering spray before the slight breeze which was coming in from across the waves. But always they went slithering back, seeming to sigh with disappointment. In fancy I imagined that they were beating madly against the restraining bluff which held them to the ageless deep.

It was fascinating; it was thrilling to a landlubber! Away in the distance the white caps leaped, danced, and died. Just over the horizon the masts of some ocean-going ship bound for the Orient could be seen, looking like the spars of a boy's unrigged toy boat. The sky was clear as crystal, and the air, coming in off that vast stretch of water, was so fresh and sweet that one's lungs stretched in order to accommodate more. And those countless, crawling, crashing waters of

LA JOLLA'S TIDES

They ripple and roll and race;
They prattle and prance and play;
　They seethe and they slide,
　They stretch far and wide,
And never seem willing to rest.

They buckle and bulge and burst;
They tremble and turn and toss;
　They come with a bound
　And strike with the sound
Of thunder and pattering rain.

They spatter and spurt and spume;
They chatter and crawl and crash;
　They seem much alive,

154

Always seem they to strive
From bondage their spirit to free.

Far out the seas creep and climb;
They swell and they sweep toward shore;
   At last they pile high
   When shoals they draw nigh,
Then topple and crash and retreat.

A restless vast host are they
That never seem tired of play;
   They race at the shore
   And seek evermore
A way from the ocean's grim hold.

My youthful spirit thrilled under the influence of the scene and my heart jumped under the spell of the mighty sea and its restless, rolling waves and sun-kissed breakers. My eager eyes sought to catch every new shift of scenery upon the stage of that gigantic playhouse. While I stood enraptured, my mind—inquisitive creature that always wants to get behind the scenes regardless of the beauty—became quite restless. I fancied myself listening to Father Time.

The Deep Sounds a Warning

"Oh, waters of the mighty sea! Would you escape your eternal prison house? Would you make yourselves free from the vast, salty deep? The Almighty has set your bounds, and He has prescribed the only way by which you may escape them. He alone can free you! You come bounding in to the shore, seemingly anxious to escape, eager to go on and on. You chafe and fret at your limits. Day after day, week after week, year after year, century after century, you break in endless fury against the walls of this mighty bluff, but you always go back, broken, defeated, salty, and more contaminated than you were when you came.

"Would you soar in the heavens above you? Would you escape your salt and silt and weeds and corruption? Would you become fit for the needs of the creatures whom your Creator made you to bless? Would you soar above yon distant mountain and, catching the beams of light from the sun, transform yourselves into a radiant promise of Almighty God? Would you roll in majestic splendor high above the earth, catch the storm king upon your breast and terrify the earth with a demonstration of mighty power which goes practically unnoticed where you now are? Would you pass out across the plains and valleys, borne upon the bosom of some midnight zephyr and, when a needy place is found, kiss the lips of the opening flowers, leaving drops of sweetest nectar in their pure hearts?

"Would you be servants instead of slaves? Would you build up life instead of seeking to tear down these cliffs? Would you be pure? Would you bless instead of rage? Would you know freedom and beauty and glory? Would you enter into the eternal secrets of the Creator and play your full part in His marvelous plan? Would you lift up drooping lives, bring freshness and fragrance into stagnant places and cause happiness to flourish?

"Then you must be born again! You must catch the gleam of the rising sun, warm up to his touch and yield yourselves to his magic! He is able to transform you into crystal drops pure and sweet! He will give you liberty! He will free you from contamination! He will take away the stain from your bosom! He will make you radiant and glorious! He will leave you free to forsake your prison house and go on missions of life and joy to living creatures! You cannot remove these stone walls! You cannot rise high enough to pass without their pale! You are doomed to defeat unless you yield to Him!"

Thus did my mind, under the spell of the scene, hear an appeal to the inanimate waves as if they had been living sentient creatures. I stood with bared head, facing the wind and reveling in the glory of the dying day. When at last the sun had sunk to the rim of the sea, leaving a long streak of copper across the waters, I sat down and, with eyes upon the lashing surf below me, gave way to musings:

Are you tired of the way you've been going?
Is there pain or distress in your soul?
Would you feel the delight found in knowing
How to mount to your God-ordained goal?
Then be wise! Heed God's clear invitation;
Let His Son touch your soul, make it live!
He alone can bestow full salvation
And from sin's sordid bonds freedom give.

Does the wild, restless sea have no meaning
When its mad rushing waters you see?
Will you go blindly on, ever leaning
On your own futile will to be free?
Hear the voice that is tenderly pleading,
"Yield to me and your soul shall be pure.
Follow me! Trust my Spirit's wise leading
And you'll find God's eternal sin cure!"

Lift your eyes! See the hills! Let tomorrow
Challenge you from the world to be free!
Let not sin's sorry blight bring more sorrow,
Make more grim days that yet are to be.
Take your soul unto Christ and He'll make you
Like washed wool or the new-fallen snow;
Yield your will unto Him and He'll take you
To the realms where true freedom you'll know.

At last, when the wind had fallen asleep and shadows were creeping in thick from the East, I reluctantly drove away from La Jolla and its fascinating caves and waters. I reached San Diego and passed through to the bare hills beyond. There in the quietness of the then open semidesert I had more time to meditate, and my mind returned to the restless waters and the lesson which Time had given me through them.

157

The very definite implications of Father Time's message to the waters of La Jolla spurred me to begin a more careful study of the subject of regeneration. I have pursued it off and on through the intervening years since that pleasant afternoon. In this study I have found that Nature backs up the Word of God in support of the contention of Jesus to Nicodemus, "Ye must be born from above" (John 3:3 R.V.).

1. Nature's Message. Everyone is somewhat familiar with the figure of the crab apple, like unto the illustration found in Paul's words regarding the grafting of the Gentiles into the stock of Abraham (Rom. 11:17–24). There is no way yet known by which the crab apple nature can be materially changed. One can cultivate it, develop it through selective processes, and thereby produce larger and more attractive fruit; but the sharp, biting acid and woody pulp will still make it unpalatable. If one wants luscious fruit from a crab apple he must take away the native stock and substitute for it stock that contains a different nature.

Or consider a small piece of steel, a needle of certain shape and size. It is an inanimate thing and, unless moved by an outside power, will continue where it is until it rusts away. But, let it be filled with that mysterious energy which man has named magnetism and what happens? It takes on life, for a new nature has been given it. Put it upon a pivot from which it may swing and immediately it moves of its own accord, turning its positive pole toward the North Star. Why it does that, why magnetism will not operate in some other medium, how the energy takes hold of the steel needle, none can explain.

Even so does the Spirit of the living God make something new out of the human life into which He is allowed to enter and over which to hold sway. Jesus sought to get Nicodemus to see what He is still trying to get the world's scholars, yes, all others to see: by nature man is a sinner (Eph. 2:3; Rom. 3:19–23); the human spirit is dead because of sin (Rom. 5:15; II Cor. 5:14;

Eph. 2:1); man is alienated from God (Eph. 2:12; Col. 1:21); he cannot free himself from his spiritual death, his helpless condition (John 3:3; Ps. 49:7; Eph. 2:12); his carnal mind cannot accept simple truths about God and other realities of the spiritual realm (Rom. 8:7; Titus 1:15; Col. 1:21).

But let the Spirit of God come into one's life and a transformation takes place! That which has been under bondage to sin is set free (John 8:32, 36; Rom. 6:18, 22; 8:2; Gal. 5:1); that which has been cold, calloused, and carnal in nature becomes warm, tender, and considerate (Ezek. 11:19; John 13:35); the old nature which spurned God is taken away and a new nature is substituted, so that one hates evil, even that which crops out in his own flesh (Rom. 7:14–25); instead of using the titles of Deity in profanity, the new man cries with reverence and devotion, "Abba, Father" (Rom. 8:14–16); and, all doubts regarding the deity and lordship of Christ having been removed, the believer can shout with Thomas, "My Lord and my God!" As surely as the new bud, grafted into the crab apple stem, draws from old roots resources which are transformed into good fruit; as surely as magnetism in a steel needle draws its point to the North Star; so surely does the implanted Spirit of God change the conduct of the sinner and turn him toward the future with a new outlook in his soul and a new dynamic in his nature.

There is much mystery in the new birth, even as Jesus indicated to Rabbi Nicodemus. He, like all other unregenerate people do, sought to interpret a great spiritual truth through human experiences and in human terms. Jesus, however, led him to realize that he was dealing with something too subtle for such a method of reasoning. One may apprehend natural truths by logic, but he must go further to grasp great spiritual truths. The Hebrew scholar was assured that the change from nature to grace which enables a rational being to enter the realm of the kingdom of Heaven is as mysterious as the going of the air currents, as intangible in its ministry as the passing of the wind.

Jesus did not use the expression, "Be born from above," unadvisedly. The greatest mystery in the natural realm is the development of a human being from a microscopic spark of life into a normal baby's body and the coming of that body into the world, occupied by a creative spirit. No one can explain the process of procreation, except to call attention to certain physical aspects of it. How the factors which determine the complexion, size, shape, disposition, and other things which go to make human beings, can be compressed into the compass of one infinitely small speck of life is a sublime mystery. But no one denies it because he cannot explain the *all* of it! Then why, when eternity is involved, will men be foolish enough to refuse to consider the mystery of the new birth merely because they cannot grasp with their minds the problems involved therein?

2. *God's Direct Word.* There is an undeniable, inescapable need both for the incarnation of Christ to be Redeemer and for a new birth. The mystery of the incarnation is not found in Christ's birth of the virgin; it lies in the very nature of God who is Father and Son and Holy Spirit in one person. The new birth is not determined by a natural event, as Nicodemus falsely surmised. Neither is it dependent upon a human institution nor limited to any race or class; it grows out of the purpose of God who, having created man after His own, divine image, clean and noble and upright, and having witnessed his sorry state caused by sin, yet "is not willing that any should perish but that all might be saved" (II Peter 3:9). One must not be misled into seeking the means of salvation among things which fallen man has produced; he will find them only by going to the Author of salvation, Jesus Christ the Creator and Lord. What does His Word reveal about the matter? Let us again hear Father Time!

"One is never a child of God by the natural birth," the preacher cries with all history bearing witness; "he is only the handiwork of God, the creature of His making. God does not beget spiritual offspring by or through a natural birth, as some foolish people have believed in all ages. He creates each soul that occupies a human body, using natural means in providing

160

it a temporary abiding place. The spirit which comes into a human body at birth is endowed with an instinctive need for God, but it gradually turns under the impact of sin from this instinctive outreach for God either to callous indifference to Him or to open rebellion against Him. Unless the child is given proper care during its formative years, the desire for God with its consequent efforts at worship will pass away as other instincts do when inhibited long enough.

"After a child reaches the age when its own rationalizing has become dependable, when it has learned quite clearly what God's Book—not fallible men—has to say about life and its obligations, about the moral law and the results of violating it, about God's holiness and man's faults, about justice and judgment as well as about mercy and love—when such vital matters are learned and the mind has developed to where it can form correct judgments, it is no difficult thing to cause the child to realize that sin has brought estrangement from God, to lead him to accept the Gospel invitation, and thus to turn with penitent heart and willing mind to Christ as Saviour.

"At what age this may be possible, one cannot say. Certainly for children reared in godly Christian homes it will rarely wait beyond the tenth or eleventh year. But always, as long as there is life, one can have hope; for the invitation is unto 'whosoever will,' all the way from lovely, practical Martha, bewitching, charming Mary, and stalwart, loyal Lazarus to a scarlet woman cowering in the street and the wretched thief on Golgotha. No penitent, surrendered sinner is unworthy of consideration; nor can one go so far astray that penitence and faith will not bring the Creator's hand to rescue, and the Holy Spirit to transform that which is dead in trespasses and sins into a living, vital son of God and joint-heir with Jesus Christ!

Fellowship with God Implied

"One other lesson needs to be driven home to all Christians," Father Time continues; "and it should be sounded into the ears of all unsaved. That lesson is: There is no experience open to the human spirit so wholesome, so thrilling, so satisfying as intimate heart-to-heart tête-à-têtes with God. He has a father-nature, hence, desires fellowship with, love from, and obedient service by beings of His own kind. Whether in pagan or in Christian lands, the strange theories about God's offspring take on meaning when one realizes that they are the natural outgrowth of man's knowledge that God has a father-nature which cannot be satisfied without that fellowship from rational beings which children alone can provide.

"Every normal man, at some time during the early period of adulthood, has a definite desire to beget a child. It may be but a brief flash; it may settle into a longing that must be gratified. Selfishness, easily gratified lust, fear of the cost and some other things may deter one from seeking to gratify his parental desire. But he will most probably continue to have moments when he realizes that to have one's own offspring about him is a holy privilege. With the average woman the desire for a child is even stronger during the early years of puberty. Many a childless person has felt the sharp stab of pain caused when, holding a precious baby, there comes the knowledge that either purposefully or by force of circumstances one has been denied the joy of having such a little one.

"The idea of His begetting offspring through any process similar to the human way is too crude and too sensuous to command the belief of free and trained minds; hence, the new birth is the simple, logical method by which spiritual children may be brought to God. Thus the seed which is the Word of God (Luke 8:11) is planted in the mind of the sinner. There it germinates under the care of the Holy Spirit (John 1:13; 3:6) and begins to affect the moral nature by producing conviction of sin which in turn leads to repentance and the penitent's cry, 'God be merciful to me a sinner' (Luke 18:12). When the penitent sinner has been led to believe the Word regarding the promised Redeemer and to act upon the basis of faith which impels him to leave all and follow Jesus, then and there God the Almighty Father can step in. The law having been satisfied at Calvary, He, without violating His own justice, can translate the sinner into the king-dom—the realm and relationship—of His Son (Col. 1:13). Thus justice is respected, for sin received its condemnation at Calvary; the law is kept inviolate, Christ having suffered its penalty; the unchangeable nature of God is maintained, and His eternal love can find its reward in the generation of a new spirit which, im-planted in the human being in place of the soul that is dead in trespasses and sins, can and does assume the relation of child to Father. That is the Gospel you should have learned to know all the clearer because of what Nature, backed by the Word of God, has taught. That is the only message that can release poor sin-enslaved mankind from the fear of death and its awful sting.

"One might go on and on drawing from the Bible and from the workshop of Nature an endless array of facts, each in turn supporting the dictum of Jesus, 'Ye must be born again!' Whence came the 'pearl of great price' but from the magic power of an oyster to transform chemical elements into a thing of beauty? How explain the gorgeous plumage of a peacock or that of a macaw without seeing how a certain form of life—living cells—can transmute chemical elements into new things, without see-ing how a thing can be remade into something different? How can one look at the waving branches of forest trees, or at the billowing ripening wheat fields and other bounties of harvest time and not know that life can take that which is inanimate and transmute it into living forms?

"The discovery of the real nature of matter through the fission or breaking up of the atom has forced a vast new field of ex-perimentation upon science. Today search is being pursued which, it seems safe to predict, must ultimately result in man's having an abundance of an entirely new type of energy which in turn will take him into a sphere of activity hitherto known only through the fertile imaginations of ancient alchemists and modern cartoonists. The relative number of neutrons to each proton determines the physical manifestation which we call matter. Then, when man has learned how to smash atoms at will and to recombine their elements, he can 'create' duplicates of that which you see and know, and the dream of synthetic gold, silver, and diamonds will have come true!

"But why will man be so perverse in his will, so indifferent to his own welfare and that of his neighbor's, as to ignore all the Creator has put about him for his instruction about spiritual life? 'There is a way that seemeth right unto a man, but the ends thereof are the ways of death' (Prov. 14:12; 16:25), and poor, foolish people follow it! One can never change a fact or alter a divine law by any foolish whims of his mind. The fact that temporal life—whatever it is—can and does change physical substances into living forms should be enough to compel every rational being to know that the Author of life, the eternal Creator-Spirit, can transform that which is dead in trespasses and sins—spiritually inanimate—into something new, dynamic, and godlike, and He can make of any penitent sinner a new creature in Christ Jesus (II Cor. 5:17).

"The horticulturist sees the soil in his garden and might spend all his time brooding over its unlovely form, its slimy, sticky nature when wet, its offensive dust particles when dry. He might take it and some seeds and spend his life trying to discover just how and why the contact between the soil and the seed, under certain conditions, produces a living, growing thing. He prefers, however, to see the soil as a bed from which to produce something good for his body, or to see springing from it living forms that delight his esthetic senses. The florist, the farmer, the manufacturer—all who labor for the common welfare—might be willing to speculate about the why and wherefore connected with their products, but they are not concerned about these things. It is enough to know that by producing certain conditions one will find in return results that are worth seeking; he does not need to ask whence cometh the wind, or yet whither does it go?"

A good many years have gone by since I first began to reason with Father Time along these lines. Today my desire as I draw near the western horizon and see before me the "banks of Jordan" not many years away, is to impress upon every possible soul the message which my Saviour and Master uttered while here among men. That message may be presented through a paraphrase of Time's sermon at La Jolla.

"Sinners! you who are unredeemed from sin; you whose lives are held in the shackles of death, yet who have ambitions to rise from out your self-imposed prison to bless the world; you who are slaves of the corrupting influences that have come to you from the past, yet who often rage against your limitations and strike out at your bondage; you whom God made to bless the world and to bring to His creation the beauty and sweetness of spiritual powers, yet who give instead vanity, carnal lusts, vainglory, evil speech, and strife—would you be free from your enslavement? Would you break the shackles from off your immortal souls? Would you rise from out the sea of carnal things and go to bless this world? Would you escape the corruption of the natural, catch the glory of the Eternal in your lives, and go to touch and sweeten and renew the oppressed, the troubled, the sin-cursed, the sorrowing, the suffering, the dying?

"*Then you must be born again!* You must catch the beams of light that radiate from the Son of Righteousness and be transformed by His spiritual magic! You must cease from your restless raging and lie quietly before Him until you feel *His* power and until you can respond to *His* touch! You can never escape your prison by your own efforts. You can never change your nature by your own works. The rock-ribbed cliffs of sin and self stand between you and the future, and only the Son of God can lift you over them. When you truly repent of your sinful, sorry state, He is ready to free and exalt you! He alone can save! He alone can purify! 'Except a man be born from above, he cannot see the kingdom of heaven' (John 3:3, R. V.)."

The rock-ribbed walls of sin stand fast,
    Unmoved, defiant, adamant!
The imprisoning world, so great, so vast,
    Doth hold enslaved and impotent.
No pow'r innate since man's dread fall
    Can break her door's strong massive chain;
He who would 'scape sin's prison wall
    Must be transformed, be born again!

CHAPTER TWELVE

Death Loses the Game

I Saw Them Die

Robert L. Purdon had spent more than fifty years in the Lord's service, during the last thirty-five of which he had served as pastor of two rural churches in Washington County, Kentucky. He knew what it was to make a circuit of churches during the days when the back of a sturdy horse or mule was the only sure means of travel, and when rough roads, often along the bed of some creek, made transportation difficult and the isolation of many rural communities almost complete.

The long years of faithful service as pastor and friend, together with the responsibilities of citizenship and of providing for a large family, had taken their toll and he was ready to "cross the bar." He had called his children about his bed and given them his parting admonition and advice. Then he fell asleep and rested for some time, after which he awoke and made an effort to lift himself to a sitting position.

He realized immediately that he could not get up so settled back upon his pillow with a sigh. Then a strange expression came upon his face, and he turned to those who were in attendance upon him and declared himself ready and anxious for

THE GRIM REAPER WILL FALL

the great adventure called death. "To me," he said, "it is just as if I were going through a door. I am here in this room now, but it is just a step into the presence of God my Father and Christ my Saviour.

"I want to be patient while awaiting God's time," he continued after a brief pause, "but I am so very anxious to see my Saviour face to face and to thank Him for all He has done for me."

He paused again as if resting, his eyes closed and his body relaxed. No one in the room could have doubted that he was thoroughly rational. There was not one bit of evidence that he was either emotionally upset or irrational. His loved ones who were in the room afterwards testified that his mind was as clear as his body was quiet and composed.

The clock ticked off the seconds, some one hundred and twenty of them. Then, according to one who was present, "The tired eyes were opened again; he looked upward, his eyes shining with an unnatural light, his whole countenance glowing; then, after a moment, he said to his wife who sat beside him, 'Oh, do you see that beautiful light?'

"For several minutes he gazed in rapture, his face lighted with a radiance never before seen by those who watched. Finally he said again to his wife, 'Don't you see that wonderful light?' When she told him she could not see it, he said, 'I do wish you could, for it is so very beautiful.' "

He lived for eighteen hours after this incident, and during that time called attention more than once to the light. Once after it had appeared to him, he exclaimed, "It is that strange light again," and then he spoke anew of the great joy that was awaiting him.

Brother Purdon was a man of unusual culture for his time. Among all those who lived in his part of the Blue Grass State there was none more honored or more influential than this simple, consecrated minister of the Lord Jesus Christ. The story of his passing came in connection with the funeral which I was asked to conduct. It was retold during January, 1946, by the beloved minister's oldest daughter, Mrs. Murphy, of Springfield, Kentucky, who remembered very clearly the occasion, "when Father saw through the veil to where the Light of the World is waiting."

On another occasion, a cold bleak day in February in the little town of Allene, Arkansas, a young woman of eighteen was dying in the home of a local merchant and his wife, Mr. and Mrs. Curry W. Wright. They were in the niece's room along with the physician who had done his best to save her from the ravages of an epidemic which was sweeping the community and taking a heavy toll of lives.

"Few people ever have such an experience as that which came to us that morning," the Wrights later declared. "Annie called us about her bed and assured us that the end was at hand. She urged us not to grieve over her going and gave us a message for her parents who were anxiously tending six other seriously ill children in their home two miles distant in the country. Then the dying girl turned to Dr. Cook and pleaded with him to turn from sin and give his heart and life to her Saviour, assuring him, 'Nothing else can count when you come to the brink of the grave.'

"Sensing the fact that we thought her to be irrational, she stopped suddenly and exclaimed, 'Please do not think that I am out of my head; I was never more sane in my life.'

"She was quiet for a few moments, then softly sang a stanza of her favorite Gospel hymn,

> Shall we gather at the River,
>   Where bright angel feet have trod;
> With its crystal tide forever
>   Flowing by the throne of God?
> Yes, we'll gather at the river,
>   The beautiful, the beautiful river;
> Gather with the saints at the river
>   That flows by the throne of God.

"When she finished singing the stanza and chorus," continued Mrs. Wright in relating the incident some time later, "she lay for several minutes with eyes closed, and we thought her spirit was passing on. But suddenly her eyes opened, she turned her face toward me and exclaimed, 'Aunt Della, I see Grandpa and William, and Andrew, and there are others with them. It is all bright and beautiful about them! Can't you see them there?' pointing upward.

"When I assured her that we could not see what she saw, she became very serious and for some little time seemed to be in deep thought. Then she said with a note of appeal in her weakening voice, "Please do not think that my mind is wandering. I can see them as plain as I see you all.' She then described some of those who appeared to her, among them being Curry's father who died near Corinth, Mississippi, during the Civil War and whom, of course, she had never seen.

"Turning once more to Dr. Cook, she assured him that she was not 'seeing things' but knew that she was immediately to join those who had already gone before her and were awaiting her coming. It is significant that among all those whom she saw in that moment of transition, she mentioned none who had not put his trust in Christ before death came."

Several years later I talked with Dr. Cook after he had moved to Garland, Arkansas, and he reassured me, "If I ever saw a person who was thoroughly rational, Annie was one such during her last moments in the flesh. There was absolutely no evidence of raving or of hallucinations. I am persuaded that she really was permitted to do what thousands of other noble souls have done—catch a glimpse of the spirit land and those who have already gone there."

Numerous stories, similar to these two printed for the first time, could be recounted if space would permit. One recalls that of the harbor pilot of Boston, Massachusetts who died some half century ago with a radiant face and a cry of triumph, "I see a light! A great light! And it looks like the Son of God!"

There is the testimony of the great Stonewall Jackson whose last words were, "Let us cross over the river and rest in the shade of the trees." My own maternal grandmother died in great ecstacy among her loved ones. After having given admonitions and advice to them and having committed her children to her mother's care, she lay for several moments with eyes closed, scarcely breathing. Suddenly her face grew radiant and she said with vibrant voice, "You may take the world now and give me Jesus." A moment later she was gone.

Do these testimonials and countless others like them mean anything? Can one rightly attribute them all to disordered minds? When the rational being can build its wonderful air-castles, devise imaginary empires and create vast industrial enterprises out of "thin air," who are we to deny that his spirit can, under proper conditions, penetrate the veil which separates the natural from the spiritual and experience to some extent things which await the spirit in the future state? Why deny that God permits some choice souls to have before death fore-gleams of the things He has prepared for them who love Him? Why doubt that He allows some of these, His spiritual witnesses, to translate their experiences into terms which their friends can apprehend?

Such experiences of happiness, triumph, and bliss enjoyed by redeemed spirits before they leave the body have their counter-part in the foregleams of Hell which many ungodly people know during the moments preceding death. The testimony of such people to the certainty of a future sentient state of the soul is no less trustworthy than that of the Christian. The case of Lazarus and the "certain rich man" is not a parable, skeptical scholarship to the contrary notwithstanding. It is a typical ex-ample of what has been witnessed by many a true pastor during the centuries since that story was given the world by the Man of Galilee. The only essential difference between what is witnessed by man and what Jesus revealed lies in the fact that the rich man was dead and in torment, whereas the pastor often witnesses the torture of one who is dying in torment.

One morning during August, 1917, while I was engaged in a revival meeting in a small town in southwest Arkansas, a call came for me at two o'clock to come to the bedside of an unregenerate man who was dying. Two days before, he had abused me with profane words and had ridiculed the whole program of Christ and the churches. But when death began to close about his heart, his attitude changed, and his wicked and profane spirit cringed in abject terror before what he saw. The devil who had meant nothing to him became real; Hell, which he had ridiculed as the creation of preachers who used it for the sake of frightening people into giving up their money, opened its fiery jaws before his troubled soul.

He was not "out of his head" when I approached his cot that morning. He was not raving; he did not cry out in delirium or as a madman would have done. When he saw me approaching his cot, he said rather quietly but with deepest earnestness, "Preacher, come and pray for me! Ask God to let me have another chance! I'm not ready to die, but if He will give me another chance, I'll be ready. I'm mighty close to Hell and, God help me, I don't want to go any farther!"

It was an extremely hot night, and his loved ones had taken him into the back yard. The scene is indelibly etched upon my memory—the cot, the sick man, the attendants, and the stately young pines there in the dim light given by a waning moon and a smoke-soiled lantern. Beside the sick man stood two lovely young women from a distant city, his daughters. At the foot of the cot stood a neighbor, who was there to help.

I sat down beside the sick man, took his fevered hand in mine and began to talk to him. I quoted familiar promises of God and gave a brief explanation and application of these. After several moments had passed, I led in prayer and then pressed for a decision from the man who showed strong evidence of penitence. But to my plea that he turn from his past and place himself in the keeping of Christ, he replied, "It's too late for me to do that now; I can't ask God to forgive me now; but if He will let me live longer I will take care of it when I am well."

Explain it how you will, the prayer offered that night brought a change. The next morning he was decidedly better and within a few days had had a remarkable recovery. He became well, but he did not keep his vow to the Lord. In a few months he was back at his former wicked ways. He was soon stricken again and died within a few hours, his soul already in torment and without a chance to call a preacher.

It has been my unpleasant duty to minister to several victims of delirium tremens. I have talked with a good many ministers and with several physicians who also have been with such patients. I have never yet seen nor heard of a victim of this dread disorder who was not harassed in his soul by some evil. Snakes, vermin, toads, imps, devils—these come to torment one whose mind has been upset by alcohol, but whose ability to reason has not been entirely destroyed. Likewise are they present in many a case when the spirit of a sober but wicked person is ready to leave its tenement of clay. I have never heard another human cry which for sheer tragedy and heartbreaking pathos could equal that of a few unrepentant sinners to whom I ministered at the time of death which came while they were in full command of their senses. Thus the unregenerate, as well as the saved, bear testimony to the certainty that the soul is not the same as the flesh, and that it remains rational, conscious, and sentient often during and always after death.

From the days of my childhood until this writing, evidences have accumulated in support of the age-old, race-wide conviction that death does not end the existence of human beings. The crude pagan ceremony of providing food for the departed loved one; the elaborate ritual of a priest, celebrating some ancient rite which the believers of his age felt to be efficacious in helping deliver the departed spirit from pain, hunger, bondage, or dire punishment; the quiet assurance in a devout Christian's heart that death has not destroyed the departed loved one —these are, each and all, the same in their testimony that though a man die he shall live again. And now, looking back across the years and examining incidents and personal experiences in the light of a stern demand for truth, I hear Father Time shouting from his ageless place among men certain lessons which every child should know.

Instinct Trustworthy

"For what purpose is the creature endowed with an inner certainty about things which it has never known through the natural senses? A day-old baby nestles against its mother's breast, searching for sustenance even before it has tasted milk. A newly hatched alligator moves unerringly toward water as soon as it is well out of its shell in some sandy nest hundreds of feet from the shore line. The wild goose in a Canadian nesting ground becomes restless and begins training for its long flight southward, almost before its pinfeathers have turned into mature plumage. Starlings gather in uncounted myriads in Kentucky cities and villages when the chill breath of winter begins to move down from the north polar regions. Such things are not mere accidents produced by evolution; they are incidents inseparably related to the vast intelligible universe of which the creature is such a vital, although infinitesimal, part.

"The fact that the baby knows where its food supply should be cannot be attributed to any process of ratiocination; no thought is involved at all. It results from implanted knowledge upon which the creature is dependent for early well-being. Just why a little alligator, crocodile, or turtle turns toward the water none knows; but we do know that reason is not involved. Likewise, in the entire realm of life we find incidents and other phenomena, an explanation of which demands the existence of some mystical power which causes the reactions of the creature to things in its environment; and this something is related to or is a product of a trait or characteristic of life itself.

"Why then are men so loath to lay aside their vain conceits where the spirit is concerned? Why do they refuse to put credence in that universal and instinctive outreach of the inner man for God? Is there any less solid basis for, any less logic in believing that this outreach for God could never have been without God behind it, than there is for knowing that the search of the babe for food can be explained only upon the basis of the mother's breast? Instincts in lower animals all the way from the mastodon to tiny insects are predicated upon the prior existence of that toward which the instinct drives the creature. How utterly stupid you are then, oh, man, when you refuse to accept the patent fact that the instinctive turning of the human being in search of God can be accounted for only upon the basis of the existence of a supreme, rational, creative Being whom you in your tongue call God or Jehovah!

"On the other hand, the instinctive fear of eternal justice and the universal conviction of normal human beings regarding the application of eventual complete and impartial justice must be interpreted upon the basis of the fact that man who is made for fellowship with God knows that justice and Hell are his lot when he lives in utter disregard of the expressed wishes and demands of God and spurns the overtures of mercy which the Almighty makes to all mankind. If this is denied, the altars and sacrifices and other world-wide, age-old proofs of a universal and instinctive knowledge of sin and justice and atonement are inexplicable mysteries.

"Look at the records of the past! Yonder in a pagan land is a funeral pyre upon which lie the remains of a prince or a pauper—what difference is there in death? The citizenry are massed about this pile of wood and fagots where a significant ritual is about to be carried out. The fire is struck to the fagots and soon ignites the wood. The flames begin to leap up, while chanting priests surround the place and the awe-struck populace watch with bated breath.

"Then there is a sudden commotion at one point in the crowd.

Every eye is turned toward it, and from the throng there comes a woman—a princess, or a pauper in rags—who rushes toward the pyre, mounts through the flames and throws herself upon the body of the dead spouse, there to be burned alive because she and all her people believe that in this way she may go with her companion into the spirit world.

"See the countless altars, dotting the hills and valleys of time, each bearing mute testimony to the fact that death does not end conscious, rational, sentient existence for people. Hear their silent admonitions, each warning all men that to await death without adequate preparation for what lies beyond the grave is the height of folly. The instinctive response of the spirits of earth's uncounted throngs of people to the question, 'If a man die, shall he live again?' (Job 14:14) is a thunderous Yes! for he *never ceases to live; he merely changes the medium through which the life expresses itself.*

The Word's Testimony

" 'Tis about time the world's leaders of thought were recognizing a fundamental and an inescapable fact about the Book called the Bible," Father Time continues. "Too long has it been considered by them as an object of worship for the unlearned and superstitious masses. Too long have scholars refused to go to it with their minds stripped of prejudices which they have received from former prejudiced examiners. Today, with the atomic theory blasting to bits many of the older concepts about origins and life, one marvels that anyone could read the Bible and remain an unbeliever in its claims to having been especially revealed through chosen men of old. When modern science has proved that the worlds were framed by the Logos (fiat-wisdom, creative power, and redemptive love of God as expressed in and through the Christos) so that things which are seen were not made of things which do appear (Heb. 11:3), who can doubt that the writer of the book of Hebrews received that bit of scientific information through some supernatural source? When

177

prophecies (call them predictions if you must) written two and three millenniums ago are today being fulfilled to the letter on the international stage, who can refuse to believe that the Book is God's Word for mankind?

"Why then not accept its precepts and profit from its message? Is there anything so unreal, so irrational about the direct visions which ancient men of God had from Heaven during moments of supreme ecstasy? When the lower animals in their natural habitat are so completely dominated by inherent or implanted knowledge and react to their environment so naturally and so sensibly because of instincts, who is wise to claim that in the beginning of the human race, and long afterward, man did not possess a far more responsive spirit than he now has, hence, was far more susceptible to communications from the Creator and to the influence of the invisible, of angelic beings?

"Why question the Mount of Transfiguration in the life and ministry of Christ here on earth? Does it not fit exactly the pattern of His character, serve as a complement to His wonderful revelation of Himself unto His followers? Can we claim that the increasing number of believers in some form or other of spiritism are altogether insane in their contentions and conclusions? That much of their ritual is planned by shrewd minds and that their 'miracles' are hoaxes, no informed person doubts. But there are pretenders everywhere, and, without some basis in fact, they could not continue to deceive the public. The theories of spiritists are founded upon the certainty that death does not end all. Much of their ritual, like pagan practices, grows out of man's foolish efforts to make tangible that which his inner self causes him to know.

"Let us go with the apostle John to Patmos and there seek to examine things with unbiased minds. That faithful follower of the Lord Jesus Christ had grown old in service and mature in thinking. The days dragged by during his exile on the lonely island, and there was much time for thought, for meditation, for prayer, and communion with the invisible. Why seek to ac-

178

count for the record in Revelation by claiming that it was written down as the result of hallucinations which came to the enfeebled mind of the great apostle? Is there evidence of insanity in the remarkable manner in which he presented fundamental truths, yet did it in such a way that the most shrewd attorneys of the time could not use the truths against those who alone could interpret them?

"When tens of thousands of people have seen into the future and called attention to what they were witnessing before death separated them from the flesh, who are you to deny that John actually saw through the portals of Heaven and beheld not only his risen Redeemer but the angelic hosts and the spirits of the redeemed about whom he wrote? The passing days make it all the more certain that John was given a foregleam of some of the world's passing show while he was awaiting the time of his departure, as when he saw the messenger flying with the Gospel (Rev. 14:10) nearly two millennia before a missionary used an airplane in his work.

"Turn once more to the story of Lazarus and the rich man. Why will those of weak faith persist in classifying this story as a parable, when it bears every mark of a historical narrative? 'There was a certain rich man' does not sound like the beginning of a parable; it is the simple statement of a fact which has had its counterpart in history a thousand million times since the story was given. The entire incident is but a brief dramatization of what takes place every year in almost any part of the globe, for poor men die of hunger within reach of the tables of the rich. *Collier's* magazine back in April 13, 1946 (p. 22ff.), carried the story of lavish entertainments in our nation's capital, each costing far into the thousands of dollars for food and drink, yet some of those who perpetrated these orgies were using our secular newspapers to call for food to be shipped to the starving hosts of Europe and Asia, some in lands which they who gave the lavish parties were here to represent.

"At heart the story of Lazarus and the rich man is the story of the human family; of human greed which results in privations and grim want; of selfishness which results in suffering; of pride which brings poverty and ultimately finds its reward in supreme punishment. Lazarus and the rich man were real human beings, types of the human family, extremes in the economic sphere. Death is real and it lays all on a common level. But the after-life of the spirits of those who die is not alike, and the entire human race from the dawn of history until now testifies that it ought not to be alike!

"All people everywhere, for all time, know that there is such a thing as justice; civilized people know that there is no justice in a social order that lets one man starve while another gluts his animal nature upon rich foods and costly drinks. They see no justice in a system that lets one man's daughter spend $20,000 for a coming-out party, while girl entertainers at this sinful orgy barter their virtue for a chance to buy clothes and food! And, knowing these facts, people also know that there is bound to be retribution, hence, that death does not end conscious existence for the selfish, heartless sinner. The spirits of those who are free while in the flesh to choose what kind of life and ministry they will have must somewhere face a tribunal where stern, impartial justice is meted out to all. This, man's instinctive knowledge holds to be true, and the Word of God proclaims it true!

Crowning Day Assured

"That there is a day of victory for them who prepare while in the flesh for the life that follows death, only the materialist, the extreme humanist and the infidel would deny. Even they are not sure that their denials will stand the test of death. Paul's great treatise about the future life, found in the fifteenth chapter of First Corinthians, is the classical way of stating a spiritual truth which the human race has known by instinct for ages. 'When this mortal shall have put on immortality, this corruptible shall have put on incorruption . . . then shall come to pass

the saying that is written, Death is swallowed up in victory.'
The time is coming when that which the human creature
knows now by instinct and accepts solely by faith will appear;
when that which he now seeks in vain to make tangible will become real and can be appropriated and enjoyed.

"Shall man alone of all the creatures be made the victim
of a colossal hoax when he follows the instinctive guidance of
his immortal spirit and prepares for the life beyond the grave?
Is he to feel the lure of the future and turn toward the 'water'
only to find barren desert before him? Is he to stretch toward
Beulah Land, lay aside the things that handicap his spirit and
make preparation for the journey, merely to find that his inner
light, unlike that given lower creatures, is a will-o'-the-wisp,
and that the journey ended forever just where instinct taught
him to feel it was to begin?

"Let no one deceive you, O son of man!" Father Time pleads,
"implanted knowledge is often far more trustworthy than any
knowledge which man may think to gain through his investi-
gations. Where are the scientific theories that were once taught
to students as inescapable, undeniable facts? If Aristotle were
to step into the biological laboratory today, would he not soon
deny that life is generated spontaneously as he once taught?
What scientist today would defend the ancient flat-world hypothesis which for ages was proclaimed by scientists as absolute truth? Who of you who studied in universities when this
century was yet young can forget the ponderous lectures which
were heard in science classes about the atom? Who does not recall with a smile the collection of little balls, arrayed upon
stems, used to illustrate the structural form of matter? But what
has the atomic theory or hypothesis done for all that 'scientific
truth'? It has relegated it to the growing scrap heap of discarded hypotheses, each of which was once upheld as inescapable fact.

"The fickleness of man's imagination, the faultiness of his
processes of ratiocination, and the gullibility of the most highly

educated are nowhere more in evidence than in what is called the Field of Natural Science. Examine it all, oh man! and then ask yourself, 'Who is more foolish; he who puts his trust in the knowledge which is implanted through the Creator's will or he who puts his trust in what his poor, fallible fellow-man calls knowledge? Who is the more sensible: he who accepts the fact of creation by the fiat of an eternal, intelligent Spirit, or he who accepts man's variable, fickle, oft-changing efforts to explain his own creative spirit without recourse to Deity who alone can account for order, harmony, continuity, and such in the intelligible universe? Surely, it is far more sensible to rely upon the inner store of knowledge which points to God as the author and finisher of one's faith than it is to believe that any mindless energy can account for what we see and know and are.

"The Almighty Creator has not left man ignorant of his future any more than he left the lower creatures ignorant of things upon which their lives were and are dependent. The baby of all mammals turns instinctively to where its food is provided by Nature. Proofs pile up in the biological laboratory of the world. The lower creatures everywhere follow the inner source of information, and that never deceives them! Do not fear that it is deceiving you when it leads you to accept the revelation of the Book about your soul.

"Men instinctively turn toward some invisible, supernatural power which they know is responsible for what they see and experience. The inner urge for fellowship with the Creator is not the result of superstition; it is as old as the human family; it came with the first man. The grains of wheat push themselves from the stem of the plant out into the light where they may be made fertile and thus continue the life process. The twigs are always in the air, the roots in the ground, not because of thought but because of implanted character traits. Likewise the inner nature of rational beings makes them know they were not created for time alone, and that the body does not constitute the only medium through which existence is to be known and manifested.

"Here and there, across the ages, the Creator gives occasional choice souls the privilege of seeing in advance of the hour of death some of the beauties and glories of the place prepared for those who love the Lord, which they will enjoy in the ages to come. Here and there, so as to provide ample warnings for recalcitrant souls, the Creator allows occasional wicked people to see beyond the curtain and to bear witness, while yet in the flesh, to the reality of Hell; to see that unswerving, inviolable justice will exact her dues of all who live after the flesh, thereby spurning the higher purposes of rational existence and denying the Creator the use of their talents in the great program of 'having dominion over all the earth.' These evidences are given to back up and bring assurance to the inner man who has been created with an inescapable conviction in his nature that death does not end all.

"You declare, 'God is' and the earth's uncounted millions answer, 'Amen! That is so!' The infidel sneers, 'There is no God other than impossible creatures imagined by primitive souls. But testimony of Nature supports the millions around the earth and proves that he is wrong. You declare, 'God made the heavens and the earth,' and nearly all mankind joins you in your assertion, lifting their eyes in instinctive recognition of the fact that the Creator is higher than man and, therefore, worthy of man's best. The infidel denies that Nature demands the prior existence of a Creator, and from tens of millions of mouths comes a stream of questions about origins, forms, order, utility, sequence, continuity, beauty, harmony, and such, to not one of which can the materialist furnish a reasonable answer.

"The expectation of the creature is a reliable source of information. It is not the result of experiences that left their impress upon the nerves of any family group; it is the result of creation itself—the expectation growing out of the purpose to be served

183

by the creature. Since man was created for fellowship with the Almighty in the endless task of creation, it is as natural for him to seek to know God and to devise ways and means of worship and fellowship as it is for the turtle to go to the water for which it was made.

"The big thing then, is to be ready for the time when the earthly chrysalis will be cast aside and the spirit within the flesh will rush into the realm for which it was created, when 'that which draws from out the boundless deep' will indeed call one home and that which is made in the image of God may return to God, shriven and prepared for personal, intimate contacts with Him and all others worthy to be in His presence. He who is wise will shine as the stars forever and forever; he who is foolish enough to believe that physical death is the end of his all will suffer the damnation which folly creates for all her dupes.

"Be wise, therefore, and turn a deaf ear to all who would make you doubt the validity of the testimony which your inner self gave you before men of the schoolrooms, wise in their own conceits, turned loose against your immature and untrained mind the questions which may as readily be answered in the affirmative as in the negative, since the answers must forever be based upon one's own attitude of mind and heart. 'How did God arrive on the scene? Where did he get the things from which He made the world? Has anyone seen God? Where does God reside?' These and other inquiries may be raised, and finite minds, handicapped by lack of data from the ages, cannot answer them with dogmatic certainty. But how much less possible is it for the skeptic to deny, with cold, scientific facts to back his assertions, when the believer declares, 'I know that my redeemer liveth . . . and though after my skin worms destroy this body, yet in my flesh shall I see God, whom I shall see for myself, and mine eyes shall behold, and not another' (Job 19: 26, 27)? Surely countless ages of experience and countless testimonies from the past should make you willing to trust the inner voice!"

DEATH NOT THE END

Is there nothing to faith but delusion?
Is one's hope but a shadow that flies?
Is the light of one's life but a phantom
That will fade from his presence who dies?
Does the instinct for God have no meaning?
Is it baseless and useless and vain?
Can poor man not rely upon visions
Of the land where there's nevermore pain?

Why disturb your poor heart with such questions?
Why let problems like these move you so?
Hear the voice speaking out from within you,
Telling all, everywhere, they can know
That the soul does not end with one's dying,
Nor life's flame lose its glow at the grave.
Dust to dust must return each man's body,
But to God goes the soul that He gave.

Death on earth is no bar to the future;
It can ne'er put an end to man's way.
There's no sense in becoming a victim
Of most fears that one meets every day.
Be assured by the light that's within you—
'Tis a light shining aye through the gloom—
That your faith points the way unto Jesus
Who will banish all fear of the tomb.

Oh, the joy when one knows that his being
Is not done with earth's short, sin-filled day!
How his heart leaps within for sheer gladness
When the truth about God holds full sway!
There's no fear for the soul that trusts Jesus;
Faith and hope then are made full and whole.
Lift your heads! Calm your hearts! Shout for gladness
All who yield to the lift of the soul!

185

Shun the doubts! Spurn the fears, O, believer!
This old world needs a dogmatic word
In support of the claims of the prophets
Who have told of the Day of the Lord.
Tell of Heaven and gladness awaiting
All who follow the Truth and the Way;
Throw your all on the altar of service
And await with delight that great day!

The Sickle Breaks

"When you declare that God is and that He is a rewarder of them who diligently seek Him [Heb. 11:6]," Father Time says in conclusion, "be sure to know that no living soul can deny categorically that you are right. He cannot back his denial with any stronger evidence than that upon which your own faith or conviction rests. When you turn by instinct to follow the inner light that came into the world with your flesh, and find in the Bible evidences that support your convictions about immortality and about the reality of God, never be afraid to trust them, for no man can bring against them any stronger arguments or nearly so much true scientific data as you can furnish in support of them.

"Whether you espouse rationalism in its denial of spiritual facts and in its sneers at the idea that man's soul lives on after the death of his body; or whether you stand firmly by the declaration of the Bible about the immortality of your soul and what awaits it in the future, know this: You reach your ultimate decision by faith and not through rationalizing. When, therefore, you trust your instinctive and your acquired knowledge about God and all that the Bible reveals concerning the future of your soul, you are depending upon dual evidences, whereas he who denies the existence of God and the immortality of man's spirit has only his fickle mind to support him; and it, if given a chance, will not accept without protest the negations

186

which grow out of faulty examination of eternal verities!"

The old sage Time closed his book, picked up his hourglass and left me. The more I have pondered his words the surer I have become that what I knew as a little child, searching out the hidden things of life and of God, was true. I have tested childhood's instinctive reactions by every means at the disposal of an inquisitive mind. I have been led to see the inseparable relation of man's creative spirit to the Almighty without whom inexplicable problems pile up before rational beings who would understand life; and dark, impenetrable gloom confronts them when they would gaze through the shadows which lie beyond the portals of death.

For me the battle is nearly ended and the "shades of the prison house" which began to close about the growing boy have vanished before the increasing light of revelation. Assurances held since I was a small lad, that death is not the end, have been attested by a growing mass of evidence which Father Time has helped me to accumulate and interpret. Today, it is easy to rest under the shadow of the Almighty while the struggle between Him who is the Way, the Truth and the Life, and Satan, the Lord of Death, is waged about me. In the end *I know that the Grim Reaper will have his sickle broken and that he will finally be bound forever by the Lion of the Tribe of Judah!*

DEATH'S STING REMOVED

I'm looking toward the road's good end.
I'm waiting for the last roll call.
I'm counting days till God will send
For me, and earthly house will fall.

There's rest and peace for me o'er there
In realms where God's own children dwell;
There where no trouble, grief or care
Can come, and all for me is well.

187

Why shudder at the thought of death!
Why tremble when the end draws nigh?
Why worry o'er the hour when breath
Shall fade away as does a sigh?

Just let him come with sickle keen!
No terror to my heart he'll bring.
For since the Saviour's face I've seen
I've lost all fear of death's keen sting.

When silver cord shall stretch and break,
My soul from flesh shall be set free;
From death's grim sway my flight I'll take
To deathless realms prepared for me.